# PUMPKINS
### *and* PETUNIAS

# PUMPKINS
## *and* PETUNIAS

---

## Things for Children to Do in Gardens

---

By:

## Esther Railton-Rice
## and Irene Winston

**To order additional copies of this book, contact:**
Xlibris LLC
1-888-795-4274
www.Xlibris.com
Orders@Xlibris.com
126633

# Contents

## <u>Dedication</u>

For Naomi Winston, Zachary and Adeline Wallace, and all the children who are fortunate enough to play in gardens.

# Foreword

If you have searched for a well-written book to guide children in an exploration of their outdoor surroundings, it is my pleasure to introduce *Pumpkins and Petunias* to you. As a science teacher/educator with three decades of teaching experience, I have become an advocate for the kind of early childhood education that *Pumpkins and Petunias* promotes—authentic, inquiry-based, active learning that encourages educators to utilize multidimensional learning strategies that engage with a child's natural curiosity to observe, explore, play, and create in his natural surroundings.

Who better to write such a book than these two accomplished authors, Esther Railton-Rice and Irene Winston! Esther Railton-Rice is a professor of education emerita at California State University, Hayward, now East Bay. She is an internationally known professor of environmental education with experience in the primary classroom, outdoor education, and national parks and playgrounds, and I was privileged to have Esther's guidance as I completed my first post-baccalaureate degree. Dr. Railton-Rice's publications include *Teaching Science in an Outdoor Environment* with Phyllis Gross (UC Press 1970), "Teaching Arithmetic Outdoors" in Hammerman and Hammerman's *Outdoor Education* (1973), and articles in *Nature Study*. Her expertise was sought as an editor for the State of California Environmental Curriculum Guides. Coauthor, Irene Winston, a science teacher with a master's degree in botany and education, is a docent at a public native-plant garden. She wrote an activity guide for that California native plant garden plus several other articles on plant adaptations and lichens. Irene's interactive children's exhibit on lichens for the annual California Lichen Society's display at the San Francisco Mycological Society's Fungus Fair is so popular that it is repeated annually as well as presented at the University of California, Berkeley, Jepson Herbarium. Both Irene and Esther enjoy their own gardens, and Irene has introduced her two-year-old granddaughter to the delights of examining flowers, lizards, birds, butterflies, and dragonflies there.

As I read through the *Pumpkins and Petunias'* activities, my thoughts first went to my own outdoor-learning experiences. Perhaps, in this regard, I was a lucky child. My father's mother was a gardener, and my mother's father was an explorer.

Fresh tomatoes and peppers covered Grandma's kitchen windowsill in the summer; green onions rested in a paper sack nearby, and the purple rhubarb stalks became a sweet, tart pie. As a child, I didn't care much for any of these foods, but

I recall being rather fascinated at the bounty of her small garden. Had I done the activity "Preparing Lunch," I may have been more open to trying them.

Other activities such as "Will It Rain Soon?" and "Effects of Wind" conjured up memories from when I was eight and my grandpa drove me to Yellowstone National Park. It was the first time I had any recollection of being outside the borders of Illinois and the beginning of my own wanderlust. An entire new world lay before me as we witnessed the amazing effects of weathering in the Badlands, smelled the abundant geothermal activities and strong scents of a pine forest in Yellowstone, and observed elks, buffaloes, and bears. My grandpa's enthusiasm for giving me such an authentic experience sparked a lifelong ambition to see, feel, hear, and smell as many wonders of the natural world as life could afford me.

During my review of *Pumpkins and Petunias*, it became apparent that it is a book that lays the groundwork of conceptual awareness that benefits children as they encounter related concepts at more sophisticated cognitive levels. For example, "Drawing Shadows" and "Playing with Shadows" have children examining the physical properties of light. Thinking about children doing "The Garden Air," "Comparing Plants," and "Biodiversity" brought to mind these early, impactful experiences that later led me to study the sciences.

When my own children were young, my wife and I endeavored to support what came naturally to them by providing opportunities to explore the environments they encountered in their daily lives.

My older daughter loves to garden; we love to travel. One summer, while working for the US Forest Service in Idaho, my wife and daughter joined me to camp for several days. I have a wonderful memory and picture of this little seven-year-old sitting in an outhouse, holding a bouquet of wildflowers she had just picked, enjoying their fragrances. Today that same little girl still loves flowers and plants (although she avoids outhouses). When she was small, we planted seeds in our tiny backyard garden and watched as they grew into fragrant flowers and tasty foods. Along the way, she encountered tomato worms, aphids, bees, and other insects, not to mention rabbits and birds. What a treat it was to watch all the interactions in that little garden. Those early outdoor experiences shaped who she is today.

Many children don't have the same chance to travel or have a garden at home, but nearly all can visit their school grounds and gardens. And ask any child, and she'll tell you about the excitement that comes from a simple trip outside the classroom.

One of the reasons *Pumpkins and Petunias* is such a great resource for teachers and parents is because the scope of opportunities its multidimensional activities provide children encourages them to explore and investigate the world that they live in every day.

The activities are organized thematically by age and, important for teachers, have been aligned to many areas of common core curricular and early childhood education standards. They employ effective learning strategies using exploration and observation, tactile investigation, creative activity, and symbolic representations that attend to multiple intelligences. The students build skills (data collection, measuring, recording, prediction, communication, and more) that they will use as they progress through school and into adult life. I know you will enjoy using this book as a teaching resource, and more importantly, children will be seamlessly engaged in multimodal learning that will encourage them to enjoy and respect nature to prepare them to be future stewards of their planet.

David Nickles, PhD
Coauthor, *Health, Science and Safety in the Elementary School*
Oakland, California
2013

*Dr. Nickles held positions as assistant professor of education at California State University, East Bay, adjunct faculty and secondary science credential coordinator at California State University, Long Beach, and director of research communications and outreach at the Naval Postgraduate School in Monterey. He has recently retired to Abruzzo, Italy, to tend his own garden and continue his explorations of the outdoor world.*

# **Acknowledgments**

The authors are grateful to the teachers who contributed to this book. Initially, outstanding teachers from the San Francisco Bay Area originated most of the ideas and used them with their own students. Two of the teachers, Susie Bellone and Dandel Cano, selected and edited the ones they considered to be most useful. Barbara Segal, an outstanding kindergarten teacher, checked several of the activities and added suggestions that enriched them. It is true that similar activities were sometimes grouped together to make one composite; therefore, the authors have not listed the names of all the teachers from whom ideas were drawn.

We deeply appreciate those who helped illustrate the book. Gretchen McCondochie of Kensington, California, made the drawings. Jackie Sargent of Newark, California, took the photograph of the child lying in the field of daisies.

Susan and Christine Austin painstakingly reproduced the useful appendices that match the things to do with educations standards.

# __Introduction__

On a lovely, warm-lighted October day, two-year-old Naomi played in her garden that her dad had designed and planted. There were rows of heirloom tomato plants with fruits of yellow, orange, and red colors and of various shapes—sausage, globe, or long. Naomi kept picking tomatoes and insisting that her grandmother taste them. Interspersed between the tomato plants were cosmos, zinnias, basil, artichokes, coreopsis, corn, and poppies. Fig, pear, espaliered apple trees, and various squashes bordered the outer perimeter of the garden. As her grandmother Irene and her friend Dana sat at the garden table, they watched Naomi meander around and gaze at spider-webs near the apples. Her eyes followed birds, dragonflies, and butterflies—white, yellow, and blue—in flight across her garden. She stood still and watched in fascination. Then she tried to chase the flying butterflies. She waved her arms, mimicking flying birds. They watched as bees were settling into brilliant large canary yellow squash flowers on climbing vines. Dana picked Naomi up, and the three of them, heads close together, observed in silence the bees moving and buzzing about in a large squash flower. Naomi's fascination with all the living things in her garden reminded Dana and Irene of how precious the curiosity, awe, wonder, and delight of children are.

## For Whom Is the Book Written?

*Pumpkins and Petunias* provides ideas to anyone who wants to spend time in a garden with young children. It is of use to parents, preschool and primary teachers, day-care attendants, Head Start program leaders, and grandparents.

It is often the case that a garden is in place and belongs to the public or someone else and children are not allowed to remove plants or parts of plants. There are many stories in which a young child attempts to delight a loved adult by bringing in the stemless flowers of a prized plant, or child, unfamiliar with flower gardens, amuses himself by popping off all the flower heads as he walks along. In another case, a field trip leader had just released a group of inner city children. As soon as they were released from the bus, they piled out and immediately began uprooting all the perennials they had come to see. After calling a halt, the leader picked up one uprooted plant and showed the children how important each part was to the plant and why the plant was important. After that, the children were eager to get the plants back in the ground before the roots dried out.

For young children, being outdoors should always be for enjoyment and fun. Nevertheless, the activities are tied to the standards for the subject areas and for early childhood education. At the end of the book, several pages of matrixes connect the activities with the standards developed by the professional groups in each field. Each activity is followed by suggestions for integrating subjects for interdisciplinary learning.

## Garden Activities Implement the Current Standards for Education

On February 13, 2012, President Obama, during his FY Budget speech, stated that there is an urgent national priority of strengthening education with a curriculum that incorporates STEM education to maintain and raise the country's economic standing. STEM stands for science, technology, engineering, and mathematics. The curriculum needs to involve problem solving, discovery, and exploratory learning. Students need to engage actively and find solutions to situations.

Environmental education "teaches children and adults how to learn about and investigate their environment and to make intelligent, informed decisions about how they can take care of it" (North American Association for Environmental Education, NAAEE).

*Pumpkins and Petunias* offers a melding of interdisciplinary environmental educational activities that incorporate STEM, Common Core State Standards, and National Association for Education of Young Children (NAEYC), and Next Generation Science Standards. The activities give students opportunities for discovering, observing, asking questions, counting, exploring, describing, comparing, communicating, predicting, measuring, recording, using everyday materials, experimenting, watching things change, creating, and the process of finding information. *Pumpkins and Petunias* offers environmental education activities that incorporate the new frameworks' philosophy for curriculums. These activities focus on how to approach and solve problems rather than memorizing facts. The method of questioning is consistent with the inquiry approach to learning.

*Pumpkins and Petunias* provides an integrated approach to teaching and learning in which language, social development, health and the arts are taught in combination with science and mathematics. The environmental educational activities include STEM elements as well as traditional activities in the *arts*.

## What Kinds of Gardens Are We Talking About?

For the purposes of this book, a garden is a cultivated or man-made arrangement of plants. The plants may be of any size. Included with the plants are all the associated forms of soil, water, and fauna. That includes, among many things, algae and oaks, microbes, and not-always-welcome deer. Although there are indoor gardens, the activities to follow are mostly suitable for outdoor areas—a community garden with several plots tended by different families; a farm garden that is machine-cultivated and that supplies most of the food for a household, school or other public gardens or nurseries; a landscaped patio or individual homes that have lawn and garden space; a small plot next to a classroom door; or even a roof garden. The landscaping in office parks is little used except for curb appeal, but these gardens can be interesting as you walk along with your children. Most of the activities in this book are for gardens that are large enough in which to do activities.

The *Oxford Dictionary* defines *garden* as "a piece of ground, often near a house, used for growing flowers, fruit or vegetables" or "ornamental grounds laid out for public enjoyment and recreation." Sometimes gardens develop a certain theme, such as a Shakespeare garden, a butterfly garden, an herb garden, a mission garden, a pioneer garden, and so on.

## National Attention to the Need for Garden and Outdoor Experience

With the current economic stress, food gardens are gaining popularity. Some of the impetus has been spurred by the encouragement of dignitaries. The Prince of Wales visited the famous Martin Luther King Junior School garden in Berkeley, California, in 2006. Former first ladies Laura Bush and Lady Bird Johnson were interested in gardens and state flowers and roadside plantings. Laura Bush advocates for children in nature and looks forward to lying on a blanket and looking at the stars with her grandchild and hopes he will enjoy "the simple pleasures of playing outside."* She quoted research that shows a direct correlation with time spent outside and achievement scores.

As soon as the Obama family moved into the White House, the country's First Lady almost immediately saw to it that there was a food plot on the White House lawn. Furthermore, the California State Education Code requires each elementary school to have a garden, and other states encourage school gardening in similar ways.

The Environmental Protection Agency, the National Wildlife Federation, the North American Association for Environmental Education, and other influential groups are working with Congress to legislate more outdoor experiences for American children.

Educators have not been blind to the need for direct experience in learning. The STEM science movement emphasizes the importance of developing a variety of learning skills through direct experience. These standards encompass technical skills, cross-discipline concepts, and ways of thinking. Next Generation Science Standards were developed in twenty-six states and endorsed by all but a few other states and the National Science Teachers Association (NSTA), the largest professional association for science teaching. Instead of memorizing facts, the focus is on how ideas are developed and tested, what counts as strong or weak evidence, and concepts that link various disciplines. The variety of activities that children can do in gardens develops these learning skills and cross-curriculum concepts. The activities in this book correlate with the Common Core State Standards and the National Association for Early Childhood Education curriculum standards.

## What If the Garden Is Already Planted?

Many times, a lovely school garden is developed with administrative support and community cooperation but abandoned when the interested and energetic teacher leaves. Once the plants are in—cultivated, weeded, watered, and harvested—most books about children's gardens offer no more. On the other hand, some gardens, like butterfly gardens, continue to grow from year to year. Public gardens and private gardens are not to be destroyed, so children may only walk around there. Or can they do something that is active, fun, and instructive? This book offers ideas to answer that question.

Young children need to play and keep the joy of being outdoors with as much of nature as is available to them. What they see may be what adults overlook. For example, a bee on a flower is something to observe for a while as it gathers its nectar or pollen and flies away. Various sizes of gardens develop a sense of space. Based on research reported by Charles E. Schaefer and Theresa Joy DeGeronimo,[**] in *Ages and Stages,* and other experts on child development, children have various needs at different ages. Many of these needs can be met in gardens.

Babies can be allowed to lie on a clean lawn to enjoy the feel of the cool earth, the texture of the grasses, the soft breeze, to look into the trees overhead and watch the branches move or a bird or squirrel scampering in them. In so doing, their eyes learn to track and to focus on objects. Often mothers put blankets under the child, but if the lawn is out of the way of foot traffic and not used by dogs, the lucky baby can connect with the earth early. If this shocks you, just watch it happen at your first opportunity. Then lie down beside the infant and try it yourself. Babies love textures. They pick up grasses, rocks, twigs, sand, or fallen cones or seedpods.

As soon as children learn to *walk*, they develop independence. They test the boundaries of the garden: Is the hedge a limit or an opening? Does the sidewalk mark the end of where they may explore on their own?

At this age, a  child  begins to want to play with others. Watching an ant can make a children shiver with excitement. Bugs are fun. *Toddlers* begin to understand consequences: bees can sting. Their attention span is very short, but this is the time to develop divergent thinking about things. They are ready to sort beans or pretty stones (except not in their mouths!) Mouths do want to explore too, so they can try new textures—the cool smoothness of a bell pepper is comforting for sore gums and contrasts the roughness of a kiwi fruit. They might want to stack a pile of fallen apples. They want to do things by themselves as Blueberry Sal*** wanted to pick berries into her own little bucket. This is the "I can do it myself" time.

Continuing into *preschool* and *kindergarten ages*, the children ask interminable questions that need so much to be answered, or else they will stop asking questions when they are older. They might ask, "What is the bee doing?" or "Will it sting me?" If you don't know the answer, it is all right to say, "I don't know," but you can say, "Let's watch and see" or "When we go back inside, we can read about bees."

At *four*, children have begun imaginative play. A beetle can be diverted by putting objects in front of it as it scrambles along. A little piece of bark can become a boat or a truck. Too many toys, it seems to the authors, stifle this creativity of making any found thing become something else in the growing mind. Language is developing, and the imaginative play is accompanied by lots of talking to themselves. "Everything has a song, everything needs to sing."***** Not all garden play is serious. This is a time and a place to be silly and, in some places, loud. Pity the child who grows up where no loud noise is ever permissible. As the children watch things grow, they learn simple sequence. Before there are beans on the bush, there need to be blossoms. Each child develops a sense of responsibility for "my row."

As children, one author's brother, sister, and she each had a row in the large family garden. They worked best out there alongside their parents. The need for responsibility was acquired as they learned to water the plants, weed the row, and above all, not step on their parents' rows! But what fun it was to make table bouquets of the nasturtiums. Nasturtiums and pansies are nice to grow because picking them actually makes them keep on blossoming.

The author watched a *four-year-old child* making her way along the curb where it wound around a tree by the parking lot near an outdoor café where her mother was visiting with friends. The little girl said a surprised "ouch" when she was pricked by Japanese flax. She grew braver and stepped into the clumps of this grass-like plant and soon found a four foot tall jungle where she could get up close and personal with a young tree. Did her mother realize that she was developing a sense of space and balance and imagination?

During the *first years of school age*, the children are more involved with others, forming friendships and feeling strong affection for others. In gardens, they can find wholesome things to do together, such as assembling a collage. Common projects help overcome the shyness that is frequent at this age.

Children have a quirky sense of humor One old poem is:

A fly sat in a pear tree, Heigh O, Heigh O, Heigh O
A fly sat in a pear tree, Heigh O, Heigh O, Heigh O
A fly sat in a pear tree, Heigh O, Heigh O, Heigh O.

Although it seems dumb to adults, that poem cracks up first graders.

At the same time, children develop fears that can be overcome by outdoor activity and, sadly in the twenty-first century, safe fences. A sudden appearance of a little garter snake may upset the adult, but if you find it interesting and know it eats only insects, that fear is gone.

Having a garden of their own, or their class's own, helps develop values for the work of others and the need for persistence over a period of time. Good outdoor manners are learned as children work along. If they visit a public garden, they learn to follow paths and not pick flowers, except with permission.

These are the years when learning to react in a healthy outdoor place develops into lifelong ways of getting high without drugs. They won't be necessary as children grow older if many interests are enjoyed while they are young. The many kinds of gardens develop all sorts of avenues to explore.

## Using the Garden as More Than a Place to Play

While current research boldly demonstrates the need for outdoor experiences and for active learning, especially for young children, recent books either address science for young children or use the garden as a place to be. The garden can be a learning classroom for all facets of early development. The activities that follow this chapter actually use the things that are seen and found in gardens as instructional tools. In other words, the garden is more than a space to do things.

---

\*   Laura Bush, keynote speech at Texas Natural Resource/Environmental Literacy Summit for Leadership and Action, San Antonio, January 25, 2013.

\*\*   Charles E. Schaefer and Theresa Joy DeGeronimo, *Ages and Stages* (New York: John Wiley & Sons, 2000), and based on the authors' personal experiences as children and with children.

\*\*\*   Robert McCloskey, *Blueberries for Sal* (New York: Viking Press, 1948).

\*\*\*\*   Dorothy Aldis, *The Complete Book of Rhymes, Songs, Poems, Fingerplays, and Chants*, comp. Jackie Silberg and Pam Schiller (Beltsville, Maryland: Gryphon House, 2002).

# How to Use the Activities

The authors collected activities from teachers over a thirty-year time span. The teachers used the activities with their own students or children, so the authors know they work. An exception is a collection of a few stories from the authors' own childhood. These activities have been rewritten to a consistent outline format for your easier use. They were chosen for toddlers to eight-year-olds. In each section, the activities appear in order of age appropriateness. However the age is not indicated because all of them are adaptable by selecting suitable parts for different ages. Many of the activities address leading children in groups but are fully applicable to one child.

Other books describe preparing soil, planting and tending gardens with children. This book suggests things to do in a garden that is already in place. Not all of the activities are suitable for every garden. For example, your garden may not have trees.

In each activity, you will find a purpose, a list of materials you may need (depending on how much of the activity you will use), a short note to the leaders with background information or cautions, the procedure, subject-matter correlations, and sometimes suggestions for follow-up. It is not intended to use all of any activity at one time but that the leader should select what is appropriate for the child and the garden at a given time.

At the end of each activity, the main subject standards that are met are indicated. Furthermore, in the appendices, each activity is matched more completely to the standards of the National Association for Early Childhood Education (NAEYC) and the Common Core State Standards.

## Safety in the Garden

Children need to be prepared before they go out. They need to understand that they are not to disturb the plants except for a specific purpose. If the terrain is rough, has contamination, or is stony, the children need to wear shoes. But if the soil is sandy, or even muddy, it is such fun to go barefoot. Everyone should know the feel of the soil and of grass between the toes. How else can we be in touch with the earth? Running in a garden is fun if there is a grassy area but dangerous if it is stony or has sharp sticks between the plant beds. The adult would be wise to crawl around the part of the garden that is to be visited to study it from a toddler's perspective.

Weather is another consideration. Coats or jackets are important if the weather is cool, raingear if it is wet. There is no need to stay indoors and miss the joy of puddles and the smell of a wet garden. On the other hand, if it is a sunny day, sunscreen and hats are important as we are learning the long-term problems of too much early exposure to the sun. Skin cancer breaks out many years later.

Plants themselves can be harmful. Warn the children about prickly or thorny plants and to keep away from poison ivy or poison oak if the garden includes a natural area. Some other plants, such as oleander and primroses, cause rashes on some people.

Therefore, it is best not to use them for an activity. Of course, it is important for the children to understand that they do not put any part of any plant in their mouth without first being told it is edible.

Children may have allergies or asthma. It may be to dust, pollen, or pesticides. They may need to have some things brought in to them until the season is past. Make sure the plant materials the children come in contact with have not been recently sprayed with pesticides. If the children sit on the grass—and they should if at all possible—make certain that it is clear of contamination and it is not where dogs are likely to defecate.

The leader should introduce tools one at a time and demonstrate their correct and safe use, as well as how to clean them and put them away. The children need to know who is going to use the tool and in what order it will be shared. It is to be used only for the given purpose, and if not, the leader has to put it away.

An enclosure is most important. Most gardens for children have fences or walls around them to contain them and to keep out undesirable strangers. If the grounds are extensive, the children must know they are to stay in a certain part. Natural barriers, such as hedges, can help designate where the group is to stay. Above all, each child is to *stay with the group*!

## **Materials Needed**

Select just the ones for the part of the activity you are going to do. These are simple and readily available and are kept to a minimum. If collecting jars are indicated, do not let the children carry around glass. Use plastic containers, paper cups, or lunch bags.

For looking closely, discovery museum stores and nature stores sell insect boxes, little plastic cubes with a magnifying glass in the lid. These are wonderful for observing insects without harming them. There is no airhole, so the insects must be released as soon as the children are through looking at them. Cheap magnifiers with plastic lenses are now available, but the practice of looking closely can be effectively taught by making a small loop of pipe cleaner or other soft wire with the twisted ends forming a handle.

For observing distant things such as birds, binoculars can be made by taping toilet paper rolls together; telescopes by using one paper towel roll. These may be decorated, and they allow the leader to see where the children are looking.

When it is allowed for children to collect from a garden, show them how to do so without damaging the plant. Leaves should be picked only from the sides of stems because the end, or terminal leaf controls the direction the stem will grow. Never pick where there are only a few of something. Pick off the ground wherever possible rather than from living things. Picking stems may pull up the entire plant. Show the children how to snap off the stem or use a scissors. Wash hands afterward. Be careful not to trample on plants. Stay on the paths except where there is lawn.

## Writing

In several cases, writing is suggested for the older children. Clipboards are easy and fun to make. Just fasten a piece of 8″ × 11″ paper to a cardboard tablet back with two paper clips. If you want to, you can punch a hole in a corner and tie a pencil to it with a piece of string. Where individual writing is planned, the leader should keep the pencils in a small box so children do not fall on them or accidentally stab each other.

At other times, the leader may want to use poster board and markers. This would be especially good for activities that you want to do together as a group. One such use would be the making of experience charts. To do this, you talk about the activity with the children. Then they tell you what to write. This can be a reaction to nature—a poem, plans for what they want to do, or more often, a summary of what they did or what they learned. Keep stories short, four to six lines. If the children are learning to read or are prereaders, repeat words and use complete sentences. For example, you might come up with something like the following:

The Morning Glory

The flower is purple.
It is growing on a fence.
The fence is brown.
The flower looks like a horn.

Then you can play a reading game with it:

Draw a circle around every place you see *is*.
Where does it say *flower*?
Where else do you see that word?
Show me where it says "The fence is brown."

Even if the children cannot read the story, they get the idea that words can be written and read back, that you read from left to right and top to bottom, that you read in sentences or phrases, not word by word.

In other cases, the activity suggests you make a chart. This teaches the children to recall, organize their thoughts, and read charts and graphs. In every case, do encourage the children to talk about what they are doing or seeing.

When each activity is finished, be sure the children pick up anything they have brought into the garden so it looks as if they haven't been there. This can be a fun pretend game to hide their activity from the elves or, as the case may be, the beginning of good citizenship habits.

Above all, have fun!

# Things to Do

# Let's Explore

## Homes of Animals

**Objectives**
To look for homes of different animals.
To understand where animals may live in a garden.

**Note to Leader**
Julie and her aunt were disappointed that they did not see many animals. They began to wonder where the animals could be. Excitedly, they found holes among tree roots, spider nests, mouse trails, and so on. Sometimes there seems to be nothing to be seen and nothing to do. This activity gives you a quick scavenger hunt that doesn't require material but sharpens eyes to what is around after all.

Look under boards or rocks for galls. Teach the children to turn the rock or board away from themselves so the animal does not run toward them.

**Objective**
Have the children explore the garden and look for ants, spiders, birds, people, sow bugs, squirrels, and snails.

**Materials**
A garden that houses ants, spiders, birds, persons, sow bugs, squirrels, snails, etc.
Crayons and paper (optional)
Flash cards (optional)

If you do the suggested art correlation, the children will need crayons, paper, and a drawing board. (See Introduction, page 24, on how to make clipboards.)

## Procedure

Give the children one thing at a time to find, or give each child, team, or small group a card with one of the following directions on it:

1. Find a home for an ant.
2. Find a home for a spider.
3. Find a home for a sow bug (centipede).
4. Find a home for a bird.
5. Find a home for a squirrel.
6. Find a home for a snail.

Then have them show you what they found.

## Suggestions for Related Activities

*Language Arts*: Tell why each one would like the home you found. Write or tell a story about it.

1. Have the children tell why each animal would like the home it has.
2. Let the children think about an animal they have never seen or have ever seen a picture of.
3. Have the children draw the imaginary animal and a home for it.
4. Have the children write or tell a story about their unseen animal.

*Art*: Draw an animal you have never seen or have ever seen a picture of. Draw a home for it to live in.

## Processes of Learning

*Language Arts*: Telling, thinking, writing

*Art*: Drawing

## Pond Life

**Objective**
To observe activity around a pond.

**Note to Leader**
Children love water. Some gardens have small ponds. There may even be a pond in the center of a deck. Little children will want to walk right in, so careful supervision is needed. If the children are barefoot or if the edge is not too muddy, the children may be allowed to fish for mosquito fishes or minnows or be allowed to dip out small things.

**Materials**
Timers
Paper and clipboards or check-off sheets for each child
Crayons or colored pencils
Kitchen strainers
Small cans
Hand lenses

**Procedure**
1.  Take a fifteen-minute walk around or near a pond. Children will wander and look at living things around the pond.

    First, allow the children to explore along the edges of a pond on their own, observing the precautions in the note to leader.

2.  Or have a scavenger hunt. Provide each child, pair, or group with a pencil and check-off sheet.

After the children begin to lose interest, ask the following questions:

1. What fish did you see in the pond? Were they swimming alone or in groups? They call groups of fish *schools*! What else were the fish doing?
2. Where in the pond were the fish? Why do you think they were there?
3. What other things moved in the pond?
4. What colors were the flowers that you saw?
5. Which colors did you see many of? Just a few?
6. If you saw just a few, how many were there?
7. What color were most of the flowers?
8. What tall plants did you see? What short plants did you see?
9. Were most of the flowers tall or short?
10. What was in the water? Did the water plants have flowers? What colors were they?
11. Did you see birds, bees, butterflies, dragonflies, or water-skimmers?
12. How many different kinds of dragonflies did you see? What colors were the dragonflies? Were they flying or resting?
13. Were there trees near the pond? Were they tall or short?
14. How many kinds of shrubs did you see near the pond?
15. Looking into the pond, was the pond deep or shallow? What color did the water seem?

**Concepts and Processes of Learning**
The characteristics of organisms
Number concepts
Size concepts
Vocabulary

**Environmental Education Strand**
Habitat

**Suggestions for Related Activities**
*PE and Math*: Divide the class into a few groups. Each group walks around the pond and times how long each group takes to complete a once-around, counting and noting more or less, many or few.

*Art*: Draw something you see at the pond: frog, bird, butterfly, flower, or dragonfly.
Inside, make a very large sketch of the pond. Let each child paste his/her drawing where it was seen.

*Language Arts*: Read a story about bees or butterflies or dragonflies. Have the students verbally describe how the living things moved around the pond area.

*Creative Movement*: Have the children show how the living things moved.

# Insects Flying on Gossamer Wings

## Objective
To learn to express metaphors while observing insects in the garden.

## Note to Leader
Following are several ideas. Do not try to do them all! This is best initiated when children incidentally become aware of an interesting insect. They are more aware of and interested in insects than most adults.

## Materials
Hand lenses
Drawing papers
Coloring pencils
Rulers
Graph paper (for recording information)

## Procedure
1. If there is a pond or running water, watch for dragonflies, damselflies, butterflies, water boatmen, bees, and other insects. Record their colors.
2. Look for aphids and ants on flower buds and on leaves and stems just below the buds. Look to see if there are aphids by the ants. (Ants herd the aphids to good, juicy leaves and then "milk" them for their excrement.)
3. Look at flowers to find butterflies, moths, and bees. What are they doing?
4. Can you find out what dragonflies and butterflies eat?
5. Describe and write imaginary ending sentences with a metaphor or adjectives such as

   a. Flitting like a _____
   b. Buzzing like a _____
   c. Spinning like a _____

    d.  Flies are_____
    e.  Beetles are_____ (beautiful, iridescent, shining, sparkling, colored, smelly, etc.)

6.  Pretend you are a fly, bee, or butterfly. Show how you would skim the ground and flowers.
7.  Gently feel some of the insects. Contrast and record whether they are hard or soft (e.g., beetles and butterflies.)
8.  Do you see insects trapped in spiderwebs? (See separate spider activity, page 35.)
9.  Lie near an anthill or a column of ants. Watch what they do with their feelers. Make up a conversation that you think they are having and write it down.
10. If there are five or more in a group, find a log they can stand on. Then change places end for end, one at a time, without stepping off the log. Avoid pushing.

**Concepts**
Biodiversity, requirements, life cycles, weather

**Processes of Learning**
Asking questions, observing, describing, comparing, communicating, predicting, recording

**Suggestions for Related Activities**
*Language Arts*: Use describing adjectives.

*Art*: Draw insects; be aware of their color and form.

# Spiderwebs

## Objective
To observe the function and design of a spiderweb.

## Note to Leader
Spiders are different from insects in that they have two body parts instead of three, and eight legs instead of six.

The garden spider is a beautiful creature and is very useful to control insect pests. Wolf spiders lie on mats on pruned hedges or grasses and have a funnel-shaped web out of which they spring to catch their prey. Brown spiders and black widows haunt dark holes in warmer climates. Children should be warned not to poke their fingers into these places. All spiders bite if trapped, but only the brown spiders and black widows are poisonous. Tarantulas crawl on sunny slopes to look for a mate. They do note bite unless they are trapped in closed hands. The leader may risk allowing a tarantula to crawl on his clothes, but I would not allow children to touch them. Orb web spinners make beautiful webs that glisten in the dew or moisture from hose spray. Jumping spiders parachute on long webs to find a new home. Daddy longlegs have a special appeal for children. Several of them may be in one large formless web, and if the web is disturbed, they all start jumping in a way that makes the entire structure swing!

## Materials
Spiderwebs (in the garden)
Plastic insect boxes (to temporarily contain the spider for a closer look)

## Procedure
1. Wander around the garden looking for spiderwebs. Where are they found?
   Why do you think the spiders put the webs there?

2.  Can you find a spider in a web? Is there food in the web?
    What does the spider do?

3.  Gently push a spider into an insect cube to have a closer look.
    Count the number of body parts or legs.
    Find the minarets where the web comes from. There are eight of
    them that let out strands that are twisted to make a very strong
    "rope."

**Suggestions for Related Activities**
*Language Arts*: Write where the spider has built its web.

*Art*: Draw the shape of the spiderweb(s).

*Math*: Count the number of lines in the spider's web.

# Let's Observe

# Will It Rain Soon?

**Objective**
To predict whether it will rain.

**Note to Leader**
The first activity simply suggests things to talk about on a rainy-day walk.
The subject matter extensions are follow-up activities after the rain starts to pour.

**Materials**
None needed for the first part

For the follow-up activity:
Thermometer
Simple rain gauge
Pencil and paper
Blue construction paper
Green construction paper
White writing paper

**Procedure**
Ask the children the following questions:

1. Do you think it will rain soon?
2. How can you tell?
3. Where does rain come from?
4. Where does it go?

Go for a walk on a rainy day in the garden.

1. What do you do when it rains?
2. Describe the clouds.
3. Describe the wind.

4. How does the garden smell different from a sunny day?
5. Where are the birds and squirrels?
6. What animals do you see (earthworms, snails, and slugs)?

7. Keep a record of daily rainfall amount for one week taken at the same time every day.
8. Record the temperature on a thermometer for one week at the same time.

## Suggestions for Related Activities

*Language Arts*: Write a description of the clouds, raindrops, puddles, or water flow.
Share poems. For example,

> Tall trees are brooms,
> Sweeping the sky
> They let down their heads
> To let the clouds by.
>
> They swish and wash them
> In buckets of rain
> And lift them up
> To the sky again.
>
> —Aldis, Dorothy
> *Very Young Verses*

*Art*: Draw sketches of the clouds.
Cut a green hill from green construction paper, cutting just one wavy line lengthwise.
Turn blue paper on its side.
Paste green paper to it.
Tear clouds from white paper.
Paste to top of blue sheet.

*Math*: Read a thermometer or a graduated container.

*Science*: Discuss the weather or the water cycle.

# The Garden Air

## Objective
To understand that air has substance and can move things.

## Note to Leader
The children can't see the air unless it is a smoggy day. Then you need to explain that they could see particles that are in the air and that they could hear things that are moved by the air (e.g., the wind in the trees). It is fun to just sit with closed eyes and feel and listen to the breeze.

## Materials
None required

## Procedure and Questions
Ask these questions:
1. Can you feel air?
   How do you feel it?
   Move your hand. Do you feel a resistance?
2. Can you see air?
   What do you see that the wind is moving?
3. Can you hear air?
   What does it sound like?
4. Can you smell the air? What does it smell like?
   Do you like the smell?
   Where do you think the smell is coming from?
   Explain that tiny particles with the odor are being carried to our noses by the air.

## Concepts
*Science*: The qualities of air.

Air carries odors.
Air may carry smog particles.
Air may carry moisture.

## Interesting Little Stones

**Objective**
To find pebbles and examine them for their characteristics.

**Materials**
Hand lenses
Pencils and paper for the leader
Balance or spring scale

**Note to Leader**
Children are especially attracted to pretty stones. They do not need to know the names of rocks at this point, except that *granite*, *chalk*, *clay*, *sand*, and maybe, *marble* or *slate* are words that may become a useful part of their vocabulary.

This activity has to do with *pebbles*, but that word is not in little children's vocabulary. You may want to introduce it. The stones in a garden may have come in from volcanoes, mountains, creeks or streams, building construction or landscaping, quarry or gravel pit, or from the northeastern states and Alaska and Canada by glaciers. Ask how the stones got here. The children will probably answer by saying, "A truck brought them." You can leave it there or explain how you believe the stones got into the garden.

**Procedure**
1. Let's look for some pretty stones. How many kinds of stones do you have? Let's put them all together and sort them. How did you decide to arrange them (size, color?)?
2. What colors are they?
3. Bang two of them together. Try two other stones. What different sound do you hear?
4. Try to make a mark on a hard surface with the stones.
5. Try scratching the rocks with a penny.
6. Can you scratch one rock with another? Try it the other way.

7. Which rock is heaviest?
8. What are the edges like? Why do you think that is?
9. Let's make a chart to show what we found out about these stones.

### Pebble Table

| Pebble | Weight | Color | Size (L × W) | Texture | Feel |
|--------|--------|-------|--------------|---------|------|
| 1 | | | | | |
| 2 | | | | | |
| 3 | | | | | |
| 4 | | | | | |
| 5 | | | | | |

**Concepts and Processes of Learning**
Geology
Describing

# Playing with Dirt

## Objectives
1. To make some soil.
2. To see that the earth is made up of different rocks and soils and has different forms.
3. To have some fun with dirt.
4. To find out that soil holds water.

## Note to Leader
Under magnification, sand is rough and irregular, whereas clay is flat, disk shaped, and slippery. That is why a sandhill is more likely to be loose, but a clay slope is more prone to landslides. If this activity is done where there is glaciated soil, the children will find many more types of rocks than if the soil is local or hauled in from one source (unless it is a glaciated source).

## Materials
Rocks of various sizes and hardness
Hand lenses
An assortment of flowerpots or cans
Small shovels
Source of water

## Procedure for Objective 1
1. Let's grind some rocks against the cement.
2. Which ones will powder? Why do you think this is so?
3. Add some sand and clay.
4. Add some shredded plants.
5. Look at the mixture with a hand lens. What do you see?
6. With a hand lens, look at some soil from the garden. What do you see?
7. What else does your soil mixture need to look like the garden soil?
8. Plant something in the soil you made.
9. Water it and let's watch to see if the plant has what it needs to grow.

**Procedure for Objective 2**
1. Walk around the garden.
2. Find some land that is flat.
3. Look for some hills.
4. Would you call the dirt *sand* or *clay* or *soil*?
5. Look for a place that is wet, dry, sunny, or shady. How is the soil different and the same?
6. Look at some samples of sand and clay under a hand lens. How are they different?

| Soil Type | Location | Description |
|-----------|----------|-------------|
| wet | | |
| dry | | |
| sunny | | |
| shady | | |

7. Was the place always like this?
8. Why did you say that?

**Procedure for Objective 3**
1. Allow time for free play with the soil.
2. Pour sand back and forth from one can to another. How many small cans does it take to make a full can? Which can holds more, a tall can or a short fat one?

**Procedure for Objective 4**
1. Fill a can with soil. The child can decide if this is to be loose or tightly packed.
2. Add as much water as possible.
3. Repeat it with loose soil, packed soil, sand, and clay.
4. How much water did each can hold? Which held most, least?
5. What kind of soil holds the most water?
6. In which kind do you think plants would grow best?

**Concepts**
Soil types
Textures
Amounts
Change
Land forms

**Suggestions for Related Activities**
*Science*: Characteristics of different soils and their water-holding capacities and the types of soils plants grow best in.

*Creative Play*: Make different kinds of soil mixes. Build mounds of different kinds of soil.

*Art*: Make pottery out of clay.

# Clouds

## Objectives
To observe cloud shapes and movements and imagine what they look like.

## Procedure
1. Lie on your backs and look at the sky.
2. Describe the shape of the clouds.
3. Do you see clouds that look like animals, people's heads, etc.?
4. How are they changed from yesterday?
5. Are they moving?
6. Are the clouds higher or lower than other clouds in the sky? Why do you think so?
7. How do you expect them to look tomorrow?

## Concepts
Motion
Light

## Processes of Learning
Observing, describing, comparing, communicating, and following instructions.

## Suggestions for Related Activities
*Language Arts*: Listen to the poem by Christina Rossetti.

## Clouds

White sheep. White sheep
On a blue hill,
When the wind stops,
You all stand still
When the wind blows
You walk away slow.
White sheep, white sheep,
Where do you go?

*Art*: Tear paper to make clouds to paste on a blue background.

## <u>Behavior of Living Things</u>

**Objectives**
To explain three ways living things reproduce.
To discover examples of how living things grow.
To observe animal behavior.
To explain the effects of living things on other living things.

**Note to Leader**
These are things you can use to occupy the children in a spare moment. You would never do the entire activity at one time!

**Procedure**
1. Find something that comes from another living thing like it.
2. Find something that comes from an egg.
3. Find something that comes from a seed.
4. Find a bird and its baby. Why do you think that is what they are?
5. Find a small and large plant of the same kind. Which one do you think is older? Might there be another reason why they are not the same size?
6. Can you find something that does not look like it was as a baby? (Caterpillar)
7. Find something or somebody eating.
8. Find something or somebody drinking.
9. Watch a bird drink. What does its head do?
10. Watch something breathing.
11. Watch something getting warm.
12. Watch something helping someone else.
13. Watch something harming something else.

**Concepts**
*Science*: Heredity, growth, animal behavior, and relationships.

**Suggestions for Related Activities**
Do a table chart and fill in the information.

Animal Eating Drinking Breathing Making a Sound Resting

1.
2.
3.
4.
5.

Other Things to Find?

## Biodiversity

**Objectives**

To walk around the garden and pick up some twigs, barks, and rocks.
To observe the twigs and rocks and count/list other living things on the twigs and rocks.
To draw a twig or a piece of bark or rock that shows living things on it.
To learn how to use a hand lens.
To become aware of small things.

**Note to Leader**

Fungi, lichens, and nonseed plants, like mosses and ferns, hold on to firm surfaces for moisture and support. They may have reproductive parts that produce spores and not seeds. Fungi are important in decomposing dead or living things, "recycling" in the food web to get their nourishment. Lichens are composed of fungi and algae. The algae in lichens produce food. Lichens are important indicators of air quality. Therefore, lichens may not be found in neighborhoods that have heavy air pollution, but you may be surprised to find them in a manicured garden. Look for twigs fallen from old trees or the shady side of a wall.

**Materials**

Twigs with mosses, ferns, lichens
Rocks with lichens
Drawing paper
Crayons or colored pencils
Hand lenses

**Procedure**

1. Examine twigs and rocks that have mosses, ferns, lichens, and any other living things on them.
2. What are some colors that you see?
3. Feel some shapes. How do the shapes feel?
4. What do the shapes look like?

5. How does the tiny plant hold on to the surface?
6. How can it live there?
7. Is anything moving on the surface? Look at it with your hand lens. Does it have legs? How many? Eyes? Is there anything else that is interesting?
8. Draw a twig or rock showing some of the living things on the surfaces.

**Concepts**
*Science*: biodiversity

**Processes of Learning**
Observing, investigating, and describing living things

**Suggestions for Related Activities**
*Language Arts*: Let the children tell/dictate or write a few sentences describing the mosses, lichens, ferns, twigs, or rocks. During the winter, read the story of the reindeer that ate lichens. (*Santa's Reindeer* by Rod Green, Carol Wright, Jon Lucas, and Clayton McDermott. Published by Atheneum, October 2, 2007. Reading age level is four to eight.)

*Art*: Have the children draw a collage of the different living things growing on the twig or rock.

*Math*: Count the number of living things on the twig or rock. Describe the shapes of these living things by filling in a table, describing them by size, feel, and color, and drawing a sketch.

## Description Table

| Shape | Size | Feel | Color |
|-----------|------|------|-------|
| circle | | | |
| square | | | |
| rectangle | | | |
| triangle | | | |
| other | | | |

## **Effects of Wind**

**Objectives**
To be able to explain how wind affects living things.
To refuse to accept an idea as fact until it is tested.
To compare two sets of circumstances related to the same phenomenon and distinguish the differences.
To enjoy looking at nature as an esthetic experience.

**Note to Leader**
Wind direction is stated by the way the wind is coming from, not where things are blowing. Fewer birds are seen on a windy day. They fly hard into the wind but sail when they are going with it. Sometimes you can see a gust blow them off course. Meanwhile, squirrels are busier than ever gathering food.

**Materials Needed**
Thermometers for each group of five or less
Wind meters
Weather vanes

**Procedure**
1. On a windy day, the group walks around the garden.
   Find the spot where the wind blows strongest and where the wind is felt least. Share these findings. Decide why this is so.

2. Ask if the same would be true if the wind were blowing from another direction. Are you sure? How do you know? How can you find out?
   Why do you sneeze on a windy day?
   Wait for the wind to change and come from a different way. How can you tell the change of direction? Wet one finger and hold it up. Now can you feel which way the wind is coming from?

Watch the birds and animals and people and some trees. How do they act in the wind?

What would each of them be doing differently if the wind stopped?

What would each of them be doing differently if the wind blew harder?

Take a large piece of tissue paper. Let the wind blow it out. Then let go and run following it.

3. Let the children observe how the wind affects plants and infer the prevailing direction of the wind by observation of the way the tall plants lean. Do some plants sway back and forth but other plants always lean the same way? Why do you think this is so?

4. Describe how the birds fly on a still day. What do they do on a windy day? They notice whether many birds and animals are in windy places. What are they doing? Why? Where do you think they went? Why do you think so?

5. What do you do on a windy day? What do you want to do now?

6. Find places where the wind is blowing the soil away. This is called erosion.

7. The leader may read the poem by Christina G. Rossetti.

Who had seen the wind?
Neither I nor you;
But when the leaves hang trembling,
The wind is passing through.

Who has seen the wind?
Neither you nor I;
But when trees bow down their heads,
The wind is passing by.

## Concepts
Wind (rapid air movement) is one factor that affects living things.
Different living things are affected by the wind in different ways.

## Processes of Learning
Observing and comparing the effect of wind on different organisms
Inferring (wind direction)
Formulating hypotheses (shelter from wind)

## Suggestions for Related Activities
*Art*: Make a windmill. Cut a square piece of paper from each corner
to ½ inch from the center. Fold each point over the other at the center
and poke a pin through it. Poke the pin into the side of a pencil eraser.
Stand the pencil upright in the grass.
Watch the wind spin it!

Draw something that the wind has changed.

*Language Arts*: Organize thoughts into sentences, vocabulary, poetry.
Make up a poem about the wind (wind poetry, conversation).

*Science*: Older children may check weather reports for wind
information and pollen counts.

*Physical Education and Dramatic Interpretation*: Create some free
movement play.

## Bird-Watching

**Objective**
To closely observe birds and their habitats.

**Note to Leader**
First graders have been known to sit quietly for an hour to observe the birds. The "binoculars" make them feel grown up and focus their attention. Also it helps the leader tell where the children are looking. Some children are nearsighted and may be less interested in birds.

**Materials**
Journal paper (to record observations)
Colored pencils or crayons
Binoculars (or two toilet paper rolls taped together side by side with masking tape)

**Procedure**
1. Sit quietly for fifteen to twenty minutes to look at birds. Talk about where they are and what they are doing. They are apt to be near running water if there is any in the garden.
2. Record or list the various birds seen. You might want to make this an ongoing list.
   Record the date and time of day. Which season is it?

Ask these questions:
1. Is this a windy day?
2. What does the sky look like? Are there clouds? What are the shapes of the clouds? Do you think the weather makes a difference in how many birds we see and what they are doing? Why do you think so?
3. How many birds did you see? Where were they? On branches or on the ground?
   Near or in the water?
4. Were the birds small, medium, or large?

5. What feather colors did you see?
6. Were the birds' songs long or short (e.g., hummingbirds, scrub jays, hawks, robins, mockingbirds)?
7. What do the birds eat (e.g., insects, worms, seeds, water)?
8. Describe one bird's beak shape. What do you think this bird eats?
9. How much do you think the bird weighs?
10. How do birds fly?
11. How would you fly? Pretend you are revving up to do the takeoff for flying.

## Concepts
Observations and record keeping

## Processes of Learning
Observing, describing, comparing, communicating, inferring, collecting data, recording

## Suggestions for Related Activities
*Art*: Draw a bird's feet, showing length and shape. Draw the bird's shape and color the bird's feathers.

*Math*: List the total number of various birds seen and estimate their size and weight.

*PE:* Try quietly to get close to a resting bird to continue observing the details on the different colors of the feathers.

## **The Garden at Night**

**Objective**

To enjoy the special sensations of a balmy night outdoors.

**Note to leaders:**

For a long time the authors considered the appropriateness of night activities for very young children. However there are balmy nights or hot evenings when lots of tears accompany bedtime. Then why not calm everyone down with a walk in the garden?

**Materials:**

A blanket for lying on the grass
Mosquito repellant if needed

**Procedure:**

Walk around or sit still with the child to feel the night air. Maybe a cool breeze will stir.
Watch the birds getting settled down to sleep.
Listen to the crickets.
Notice the flower fragrances that carry better on the damp night air.
Do you hear running water anywhere?
Lie on the blanket and watch the stars come out.
Tell a star story.
Find the biggest one and the brightest star.
Do you see an airplane flying over?
Maybe you will see an owl or another night bird.
What do you think the bunnies are doing?
Are you sleepy too?

**Concepts and Processes of Learning**
Earth science: day and night
Animal behavior
Using the senses
Companionship
Overcoming fear

# Let's Make Something

## Using Plants as Art Tools

**Objectives**
To experiment with different media in the painting process.
To be able to compare the physical differences of various nature objects by painting with them.

**Note to Leader**
The children may need help fraying the ends of stems to make brushes or cutting a pod to make a stamp or trying different strokes.

**Materials**
Plant materials collected in the garden
Paper bags
Tempera paint (in shallow containers)
Paper
Pie plates
Stamp pads with washable ink
Newspapers (to cover the worktables)

**Procedure**
First, show the children how grass can be split to make a brush, how a pod or bud can be cut to make a stamp, etc. Show them how apples, cut crossways, have a star design at the core and an artichoke, cut lengthwise, makes a beautiful design.

Let the children use the stamps you made to make designs on paper.

1. Give each child a bag and take them on a short walk in the garden to collect a variety of leaves, long blades of grass, weeds, etc. Show them how to collect by example, what to take, how to pick it.

2. Predict what kind of mark each item might make.

3. After the collecting walk, let the children sit around a table and dump their bags' contents onto the paper plates.

4. Have the children dip the tip or edge of the plants they have found into the paint and use the dipped plants as brushes or use the stamp pad if appropriate. Encourage the students to experiment with different ways the dipped plant material objects can be used (e.g., pull grass pieces through the paint and then drag the dipped grass across the paper). Also use the ends of sticks for dot painting and use leaves as block prints.

5. Help the children compare different textures. Have the children show their pictures and have the group guess which plant objects created such special effect.

6. Name the plant parts that were used as art tools.

## Concepts
Properties of materials (materials come in different forms), biodiversity.

## Processes of Learning
Asking questions, observing, describing, comparing, measuring, recording

## Suggestions for Related Activities
*Language Arts*: Let the students explain orally how they got the special effects with their dipped plant parts. Let the students write a paragraph explaining what their paintings mean to them.

*Social Studies*: Have the students read several books or have books read to them to explore how different cultures use or used these plant parts for food, decoration, medicines.

Caution: Do not encourage children to taste any unknown plants.

*Math*: Let the students describe the characteristics of the plant materials and measure their dimensions, listing them into a table before dipping the items into the painting materials.

*PE*: Play a game, actively pretending to be the plant materials and how they move in the wind.

## Falling Leaves and Bits of Bark

**Objective**
To become more aware of seasonal changes.

**Note to Leader**
Leaf and bark rubbings provide children with a permanent picture of some of the intricate patterns in the natural world (shape, texture, and color).
Children can find many geometric shapes, straight lines, triangles, and diamond shapes. Children can combine these orderly or randomly on paper. This activity will allow the children to become more aware of seasonal changes. Direct their attention to the effects of these changes on a tree and its leaves. These are effects that are so familiar that they are often taken for granted.

Collect only from the ground. Do not leave magnifying lenses in the sun because of fire hazard.

**Materials**
A variety of leaves
Pieces of shed bark
A hard surface
Paper
Crayons
Magnifying lenses
A shape chart (for reference)

**Procedure**
Take a leaf walk. Look at all the varieties of different leaves. Look at all the colors.
Watch leaves fall and blow in the wind. Collect some leaves.
Place a sheet of paper on a hard surface. Arrange a leaf picture any way you want. Cover leaves with a piece of thin paper. While your

partner holds the paper steady, rub over the paper with the side of a crayon until you get the print of the leaves.

Hold a blank sheet of paper against a tree trunk and rub to get the texture pattern of the bark. Try some different tree trunk rubbings.

## Concepts
The differences between materials, techniques and processes; how different materials, techniques, and processes cause different responses; different media, techniques, and processes to communicate ideas, experiences, and stories.

## Processes of Learning
Understanding and applying media, techniques, and processes.

## Suggestions for Related Activities
*Science*: List the names of the trees. Match the tree barks with their respective leaves. Make a list of predictions of what may be found living/depending on the tree. Look at the tree trunks for algae, lichens, mosses, insects (butterflies, moths).

*Math*: Find and draw the geometric shapes, straight lines, triangles, and diamond shapes of the leaves.

*Language Arts*: Write a poem to describe some of the leaf shapes and a paragraph for imagining the leaves floating from the trees to the ground.

*Social Studies*: Find the fruits and seeds that Native Americans used for their winter food supply (acorns, nuts, grass seeds, berries, etc.).

## Preparing Lunch

**Objective**
To make a list of edible plants found in a garden and identify the parts of the plants they eat.

**Note to Leader**
Food preparation with young children is described in detail in other books. Therefore, it is not include here. Research has shown that raising and harvesting vegetables does increase children's willingness to eat healthy food and to try new tastes.

**Procedure**
Collect the plant that is ready to eat.
Help the children choose something that is ready to be eaten and show them how to pick it, cut it, or dig it without harming plants that need more time to grow.
Decide what part of the plant it is.
Wash and prepare it.
Enjoy.

Have the children make a list of breakfast, lunch, dinner, and snacks they eat and what part of the plant they eat. For example:

### Plant Food Table

| Plant Food | Root | Stem | Leaves | Flowers | Seed/ Nuts | Eating Time |
|---|---|---|---|---|---|---|
| carrots | | | | | | |
| corn | | | | | | |
| sweet potato | | | | | | |
| lettuce | | | | | | |

| | | | | | | |
|---|---|---|---|---|---|---|
| cereals | | | | | | |
| oatmeal | | | | | | |
| cream of wheat | | | | | | |
| barley | | | | | | |
| berries | | | | | | |
| cucumber | | | | | | |
| green peas | | | | | | |

**Concepts**
Biodiversity, adaptations, life cycles

**Processes of Learning**
Observing, describing, comparing, communicating, predicting, measuring, recording, following instructions

**Suggestions for Related Activities**
*Language Arts*: Read a local history of Native Americans' foods.

*Social Science*: Read a story of the native California description of the Spanish missionaries when they set up the missions. Give the changes with what they grew and what plants they brought with them from Europe. How did the Indian diet change?

*Art*: Draw some of the plant foods you eat. Name where they grow in the United States.

*Math*: Count the number of "eyes" on a potato or sweet potato.

Sarah Elizabeth Lineberger, "The Effects of School Gardens on Children's Attitudes and Related Behaviors Regarding Fruits and Vegetables" (Texas A&M University, 1999).

Alice Waters, "The Edible School Yard: A Universal Idea" (Martin Luther King Junior Middle School in Berkeley, California: Chronicle Books, 2008).

## Seed Design

**Objectives**
To use seeds from the garden to create a picture or design.
To form a classification of seeds by looking at the different sizes, shapes, and colors of seeds.

**Note to Leader**
Obviously, this is a late summer or fall activity. The seeds may not all be collected in one day. Use care in choosing seeds that are not hazardous and be observant of what the children do with the seeds in their hands.

Eucalyptus pods are fun to find because they have a varied number of star points on them. One author loved to make tea sets out of acorns by cutting the tips off, hollowing them out, and poking in handles of small stems. The acorn caps made little saucers. When she got older, she entertained the children with a little man made of three acorns stuck together with a toothpick, with a saucer for his cap and toothpick arms and legs. These are things you can do for the children, but they are too hard for them to do.

**Materials**
Collected seeds
Colored construction paper (cut into 6″ × 9″ pieces or 3″ × 3″ pieces)
Tacky glue

**Procedure**
1. Take a walk in the garden to look for seeds on plants and under the plants and trees (e.g., thistles, garlic, anise, tomato, nasturtium, beans, corn, etc.). Arrange the collected seeds on the paper in a picture or in a design that pleases you.

2. Glue your seeds to the paper.

3. Collect five seeds from each plant and make a set of "star" seed cards on separate pieces of 3″ × 3″ paper.

4. Collect three seeds from each plant and classify them according to color, size, and odor by gluing and labeling seeds of each grouping on separate pieces of paper.

## Processes of Learning
Choosing and evaluating a range of subject matter, symbols, and ideas. Exploring and understanding prospective content for works of art. Selecting and using subject matter, symbols, and ideas to communicate meaning.

## Suggestions for Related Activities
*Science*: Make a seed classification table:

### Seed Description Table

| Item | Size | Color | Odor |
|------|------|-------|------|
|      |      |       |      |
|      |      |       |      |
|      |      |       |      |

*Math*: Measure the seeds and sort them into various groupings, size, texture, weight.

### Seed Description Table

| Seed | Size | Texture | Weight |
|------|------|---------|--------|
| Eucalyptus |  |  |  |
| Maple |  |  |  |
| Grass |  |  |  |

*Arts*: Have the children write a sentence or two describing the feel and general impression of the seeds.

*Social Studies*: Have the children list the number of ways that seeds are used by different peoples or write a paragraph about how one culture uses or used the seeds.

*Health*: Let the children discuss the benefits of eating some of these seeds, nuts, grains, etc. How is bread made?

## Drawing Shadows

### Objective
To trace and paint or color a figure from a shadow in a garden.

### Note to Leader
Drawing shadows transfers three dimensions to two dimensions.

### Materials
A sunny day
White drawing paper and a cardboard backing
Pencils
Black markers
Colored pens
Tempera paints
Crayons
Watercolors or pastels

### Procedure
1. Let the children find an interesting shadow (e.g., a stalk of a plant or another part of a plant, fence, etc.) while walking through the garden.

2. Lay the paper right on the shadow.

3. Trace or outline the drawing in black.

4. Color or paint the interior of the drawing.

### Concepts
Materials come in different forms, light, biodiversity, objects in the sky (light)

**Processes of Learning**
Observing, describing, comparing, communicating, predicting, measuring, recording

**Suggestions for Related Activities**
*Art*: Tracing, make a two-dimensional representation of a three-dimensional object.

*Science*: Notice different leaves or twig shapes.

*Math*: Measure the different lengths and widths of leaves and twigs. Describe the leaves and twigs. List this information in the following table:

| Leaf/Twig | Length | Width | Description |
|-----------|--------|-------|-------------|
|           |        |       |             |
| 1.        |        |       |             |
| 2.        |        |       |             |
| 3.        |        |       |             |
| 4.        |        |       |             |
| 5.        |        |       |             |
| 6.        |        |       |             |

*Social Studies*: Map pathways taken to find selected objects.

*PE*: Walk around the garden to select objects/shadows to paint. Play games of hide-and-seek or play ring-around-a-rosy games or have relay races across the grass lawns, etc.

*Health*: Find and list plants in the garden that produce edible fruit or other edible parts of the plants. Discuss the different parts of plants that we eat for food.

*Language Arts*: Have the children orally explain how they found the objects in the garden and how they colored or painted them in their drawings and paintings.

## Making a Collage

**Objective**
To choose natural objects and arrange them in an aesthetically pleasing manner.

**Note to Leader**
This activity may have to be concluded indoors if there is a strong wind.

**Materials**
Natural items children collect during a walk in the garden
One sheet of stiff mounting paper
Tacky glue
Camera (optional)

**Procedure**
Suggest to the children that as they walk together in the garden, they look for something that is small and pretty. They may pick it up but not break it off a plant.

1. Go for a walk in the garden with the children.
2. Each person should bring back one natural item found during the walk.
3. Everyone comes together in a circle near a table, tree stump, or a large flat rock where the collected items can be displayed.
4. Two children can start by putting their items in the center of the display area. The rest of the children follow by adding their items.
5. After all the items are displayed, the children can rearrange the items to form a new collage.
6. When the group is satisfied, each child takes a turn to glue down his item.

or

7.  Photograph the collage after changes have been made.
8.  Leave the collage overnight to see if the wind makes any changes.
9.  Photograph the collage after the next day.

## Processes of Learning

Choosing and evaluating a range of subject matter, symbols, and ideas.
Exploring and understanding prospective content for works of art.
Selecting and using subject matter, symbols, and ideas to communicate
meaning.

## Suggestions for Related Activities

*Science*: Describe the physical locations where some of the different
items were found and later used in the collage. Notice the direction
and effects of the wind.

*Language Arts*: Write a paragraph about the process of forming the
collage. Children can give an oral explanation of what the collage
looks like to them.

*Math*: Measure the perimeter of the collage. List how many different
items were used in the collage.

## Discovering Textures

### Objectives
To touch various textures found in a garden.
To know the differences between materials, techniques, and processes.
To describe how different materials, techniques, and processes cause different responses.

### Note to Leader
Be careful what the children might pick up so that they do not handle things that are sharp or nasty. Help the children, if they choose a plant part, to pick it carefully so as not to destroy the whole plant. Choose textured objects; flower petals are too fragile for this activity. If the children rub a leaf, have the underside up. Moss has a lovely texture to feel but is impractical for rubbings.

### Materials
Crayons
Paper
Garden containing a variety of resources (i.e., containing plants with bumpy bark, soft and fuzzy leaves, ferns, leaves, horsetails, twigs, pebbles, seedpods)
Pencils (for labeling pictures)

### Procedure
1. Leader shows examples of surfaces: smooth, rough, spongy, etc. Ask the children to tell how each one feels.
2. In groups of two to four, let the students explore the garden and find three different types of textures.
3. Using three different pieces of paper (each 5" × 8") and a crayon, students should place a piece of paper on one of each texture types, respectively, and rub with the side of their crayons so that the textural images are transferred to the paper sheets. Hold the paper in place carefully with the hand that does not have the crayon.
4. Have the class meet back in a circle to pass the rubbings around to all the students. Let the students guess which objects were used to make each rubbing.

**Processes of Learning**
Understanding and applying media, techniques, and processes.

**Suggestions for Related Activities**
*Language Arts*: Read stories about a garden filled with trees, mosses, ferns, acorns, maple seed helicopters, etc. Have the students write a paragraph or a poem about the textures of the garden plant pieces they used for their rubbings.

*Math*: Let the children count the number of items that the students picked up in the garden and list the items' different characteristics (e.g., smooth, rough, spongy) in a table form.

*Science*: Let the children feel all the garden pieces that were collected and then make a class table listing the items, their locations, and their textures.

*Social Studies*: Have the children mount the rubbings and present a class-book exhibit of their rubbings. Have them write their own captions using descriptive words describing the textures of their rubbings.

# <u>Arranging Bouquets</u>

## Objective

To arrange beautiful bouquets with flowers that the children have picked themselves.

## Note to Leader

Picking flowers seems to be as natural for children as breathing. Bobby gleefully brought his grandmother a bag of all her prize poppies, thinking it was a present for her. Mike snapped the heads off all the flowers he could get near—this lesson is dedicated to him.

There are too many little hands to allow the picking some of us enjoyed as children.
Some flowers are in private gardens. Some are protected by law. Children need to know they may pick only with permission.

## Materials

An abundant supply of growing flowers
Permission to take some
Blunt scissors for each child (held by teacher until ready to use)
Plastic bag for each child's flowers

Indoors:

Jars (about the right height for the anticipated flowers)
Tables covered with newspaper

## Procedure

Along the garden edge may be dandelions, violets, daisies, or flowering weeds, such as chicory and Queen Anne's lace or anything abundant. Some garden flowers, such as nasturtiums and pansies, bloom longer if the blossoms are picked or cut before going to seed. Show the children how to pick with stems long enough to reach into a vase. Some stems are tough and need to be cut with blunt scissors.

Teach the children that they must not pick any flowers without permission.

They may pick where there are enough so that the ones they take will not be noticeable.

They need to learn to be careful of where they step so that they do not destroy more than they take.

They need to be careful not to pull up the whole plant. If the stems are too tough to pick and they do not have scissors, they have to just smell and enjoy the flowers then leave them.

They need to put their flowers into water as quickly as possible.

Help the children make a pretty bouquet. Try to get all the stems about the same length. By asking questions, help them see that not all the same color should be on the same side of the bouquet, but it is nice to scatter the colors through the bouquet.

Arrange the stiff stems first then insert the weaker stems.

## Processes of Learning

Using conservation practices to pick flowers and learn how to arrange and keep them.

## Suggestions for Related Activities

*Science*: Observe plant parts and discuss the function of blossoms in seed production. Ask in what kinds of places do plants grow (shady or sunlight areas, damp or dry soil, sand, or clay). Some plants wilt more quickly than others.

Look at some flowers, birds, insects, and grazing animals.

*Language Arts*: Talk about one's day (was it fun and why).

*Vocabulary*: Learn common names of common flowers.

*Social Science*: Environmental concepts. Decide what will we do next time we see pretty flowers and no one is around?

# Let's Measure

## Comparing Plants

**Objectives**
1.  To compare ways plants are alike and different.
2.  To understand that plants provide food.
3.  To understand that plants do not always grow in gardens.

**Note to Leader**
The children are asked to feel leafy plants. If your garden has a natural area, be sure they do not select poison ivy or poison oak.

**Materials**
Chart paper
Marker

**Procedure**
Have the children choose three different plants that interest them. Ask them the following questions:
1.  How are they alike?
2.  How are they different?

As a group, fill in plant descriptions in the table.

### Plant Descriptions

| Plant name | Root length | Stem length | Leaf feel | Flower color(s) | Fruit shape, feel |
|------------|-------------|-------------|-----------|-----------------|-------------------|
|            |             |             |           |                 |                   |
|            |             |             |           |                 |                   |
|            |             |             |           |                 |                   |

Ask the children these questions:
1.  Can you find a plant that has been partly eaten?
2.  Which part of the plant has been eaten?
3.  What do you think ate it?
4.  Do you see what is eating it?

Find a plant growing on another plant.
1.  How is it holding on?
2.  How does it help the plant to be on another plant?
3.  Does it harm the other plant?
4.  Can they "help" each other?

Find a plant growing on a rock or cement (environment/ecosystem).
Find a plant that has hard stems.
Feel the leaves. Can you find one that feels soft, rough, or smooth?
Can you find a plant that is sticky? Can you find one that is prickly or smooth, feels warm or cool?

**Concepts**
Biodiversity
Life cycles

**Processes of Learning**
Observing describing, comparing, communicating, predicting, measuring, collecting data

**Suggestions for Related Activities**
*Art*: Draw flowers.

*Language Arts*: Find textures on things and describe them.

*Math*: Measurements—make and understand a table.

## Shapes

**Objective**
To find some things shaped like a penny, egg, heart, diamond, or triangle.

**Materials**
A garden that has plants with many differently shaped leaves
Cardboard cutouts of each shape for which the children are to find examples (optional)

**Procedure**
1. Divide the children into groups of two.
2. Assign each group to look for specific shapes and leaf arrangements in the garden.
3. After a fifteen-minute search time, have the children show the different shapes they have found.
4. Look for the different geometric shapes in twigs, stones, cones, and seedpods.

**Concepts**
Geometric shapes

**Processes of Learning**
*Math*: Recognizing shapes
*Science*: Comparing plant characteristics
*Language*: Learning vocabulary

**Suggestions for Related Activities**
*Art*: Hold a leaf, twig, flower, cone, stone, or an abandoned bird's nest over a piece of paper and trace the shape.

*Music*: Try to whistle/sing a bird's call or the chirping of a grasshopper.

*Science*: Find examples of opposite, alternate, and whorled leaf arrangements. Make a list of names of these plants. Were all the leaves from plants that live in the soil, or were some living in a pond?

*Language Arts*: Write a short paragraph or tell a short account describing one of the items found in the garden.

# Nature's Geometry

## Objective
To look for geometric shapes in the garden.

## Note to Leader
Plants exhibit different shapes. For example, whole evergreen trees can be seen as large triangles. Kiwi fruit seeds are circular; apple seeds are pear shaped. Fiddleneck ferns have spiral forms; leaves can be heart shaped. Cross sections of the stems of mint plants are square. Choose just the basic shapes that the children are ready for.

## Materials
Plant leaves or stems
Fruits with seeds
Paper
Crayons
Large (8″ × 8″) cardboard cutouts of the basic shapes

## Procedure
1. Group the children in three to four and have them explore the garden to find different geometric shapes of circles, squares, triangles, spirals, and hearts that plants' leaves, stems, and fruits display.
2. The children can collect a few of the different shapes and draw pictures of them.
3. After drawing, have the children meet as a group to show and discuss their examples.
4. Let the children suggest possible uses of these plant shapes. Do artists copy them?
5. How is the shape useful to the plant?

**Concepts**
Geometric shapes

**Processes of Learning**
Observing, collecting, describing, predicting

**Suggestions for Related Activities**
*Art*: Make a collage of nature's geometric shapes. Or lay a leaf, twig, or flower on a piece of paper and trace the pattern.
Dip cut fruit and vegetables in thick tempera paint to make stamp designs. Make a print using a cross section of a cut apple showing the star shape around the seeds.

*Language Arts*: Write a paragraph or a poem describing the colors, shapes, and feel of the different plant parts.

*Science*: List the names of the different plants collected.

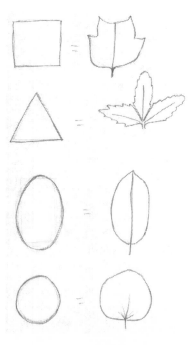

# How Many and How Big?

## Objective
To count and record measurements of things in the garden.

## Note to Leader
This may be done as a counting exercise. However, according to the
*New York Times'* Stanley M. Malowski of the Early Childhood Center
in New York, a study shows that children can recognize the number of
objects without counting them.

For example, the children might see at once that there are three each
of a flat of potted plants and so learn the number 3 (based on brain
research at the University of Buffalo by Julie Saransa and Doug
Hutchins).

## Materials
Garden with herbs and bushes
Plants that have flowers, seeds, and insects
A ruler for each pair of children (if they are older)
A simple scale

## Procedure
Choose from the following:
1. Count and record the number of flowers on a plant, the number of
   growing plants in a bed, the number of leaves on a small herb, the
   number of different seeds planted in a bed, and the number of rows
   in the garden.
2. How many of the leaves of three plants are green, brown, or
   yellow? Record.
3. Measure the heights of five different plants in a bed. Set out two
   plants each of more than one kind of plant (e.g., two squash and
   two tomatoes).
4. Ask how many birds are in a bush (if there are just a few). Don't
   insist on counting them.
5. Measure the length and width of the plant beds.

6. Measure a very big leaf.
7. Weigh a large squash.
8. How many different colors are the flowers? Record. Name the colors.
9. Count and record the number of insects and birds found in or near the beds. Were the insects on the leaves or flowers or on the soil? Record.
10. What season is this? What time of day?

## Concepts
Number and operations

## Processes of Learning
Observing, describing, measuring

## Suggestions for Related Activities
*Language Arts*: Write a paragraph to describe how the plants in one bed are different from plants in another bed.

*Science*: How are the plants adapted to dry weather or wet weather? Is there a lot of rain during the year or very little? (Does it rain often or not?)

*Art*: Draw some of the different leaves in the garden.

# Let's Make Music

# Food Chain Song

## Objective
To learn about a food chain while singing to the tune of "The Farmer in the Dell."

## Note to Leader
This singing game is a parody on "The Farmer in the Dell."

## Materials
None required

## Procedure
1. Have the children form a ring by taking hands.
2. One child is chosen to be the SUN who stands in the center of the circle and "shines."
3. The ring circles around the sun as the children sing.
4. Children are chosen to role-play the parts indicated in the song.

The sun shines above, the sun shines above,
Hi ho, the food chain game.
The sun shines above.
The rain falls on all, the rain falls on all (etc.)
The seeds grow into plants (etc.)
The duck eats the plants (etc.)
The fox eats the duck, the fox eats the duck,
Hi ho, the food chain game,
The fox eats the duck.

## Variations
The sun, the rain, the seeds, the mice, the snakes, the hawk eats the snake, hi ho, the food chain game, the hawk eats the snake.
The bird eats the worm, the snake eats the bugs, etc.
You can add in *insects, frogs,* etc.

**Concepts**
*Science*: Energy and change, biodiversity, requirements, life cycles, and weather.

**Processes of Learning**
Observing, describing, comparing, communicating

*Music*: Singing, alone and with others, a varied repertoire of music. Singing in groups, lending vocal timbres, matching dynamic levels, and responding to the cues of a conductor.

**Suggestions for Related Activities**
*Art*: Draw a food web using some of the plants and animals from the song. Make a large chart showing a food chain for the whole group and individual ones for each child.

*PE*: Do an interpretive dance of the various animals.

*Science*: Discuss our planetary system, our sun and its planets.

*Language Arts*: Write lyrics for "The Farmer in the Dell."

*Math*: Count and list the different animals sung about in "The Farmer in the Dell."

## Nature's Band

**Objectives**
1. To be more aware that music is all around them.
2. To realize that rhythm and wind are part of music.
3. To make music out of the instruments found in the garden.
4. To use their voices to mimic bird sounds, wind sounds, or other sounds.

**Note to Leader**
Sounds may be made by shaking bones in a gourd, clapping sticks together, swinging shells on strings, clapping bones from lunch, whistling on grass being held between extended fingers, rattling a branch of dry leaves, shaking a hollow stick containing a small amount of sand, shaking dry gourds, blowing over the open end of an acorn cup, or anything you can devise.

**Materials**
Objects from nature (seeds, gourds, acorn caps, dry leaves, hollow sticks like bamboo, blades of grass, stones, bones, shells, sand)

**Procedure**
1. Have the children find natural objects to use as rhythm or musical instruments. Shake pebbles together to make maracas. Strike sticks or rocks against each other or against a log. Crumple dry leaves. Shake a dry branch or scrape it against the ground. Hold a wide blade of grass between two thumbs and blow across the edge to produce whistling sounds.
2. Practice by copying beats the leader makes by first clapping a rhythm; then have the children use their instruments to play that beat.
3. Let the children demonstrate their own music makers.
4. Let the children play their instruments singly or collectively.

5. Have the children use their voices to imitate some of the sounds they hear.
6. Let the children march and play their instruments in their marching band.
7. Discuss what noise is to some and what music is to others.

## Concepts
Properties of materials—materials come in different forms
Position and motion of objects
Energy and change
Land, air, and water properties and resources
Sound made by motion or by vibration

## Processes of Learning
Communicating, predicting

## Suggestions for Related Activities
*Music*: Sources of sounds and composition of an orchestra.

*Language Arts*: Have the children describe the tone of their instruments (clicking, rattling, swishing, thumping, clashing, crackling, etc.). New vocabulary, explaining, communicating.

*Social Studies*: Native American and African tribal music is made up of rhythm. Play recordings of the music of different cultures.

*Science*: Discuss how animals use sound (especially in groups), why birds sing, why some mammals have long ears. Listen to recordings of garden birds. Share memories of animals' sounds they have heard (e.g., raccoons, coyotes, mockingbirds). Talk about dogs having different barks for different times or animals' use of sound for survival and about wind. Identify rhythm of objects.

*Health*: Music has a calming or exciting effect. Loud sounds can damage ears.

*Math*: Measure or work with different sizes and shapes of environmental instruments (spatial skill) such as elderberry whistles made by an adult and rhythm sticks.

## Musical Gourds

### Objective
To create musical instruments.

### Note to Leader
The plants represented on the table are not usually called gourds but are classified in the gourd family. You might ask the children what is alike about each one.

### Materials
Dried gourds of different sizes (small, medium, large)
Dried seeds
Pebbles
Sand
Cloth (to cover cut dried halves of the gourds so that a tympanum is formed)

### Procedure
1. Examine different dry gourds.
2. Collect and use natural objects to test sounds make by shaking them inside their cloth-covered dry gourds.
3. Create a musical gourd using one of the gourds.
4. Ask this question: Are there a few seeds or many seeds in the gourds?

### Extension
1. Examine and discuss properties of wet gourds and then remove and examine the interior contents.
2. Add data to a table of characteristics regarding color, size, shape, and weight of gourds.
3. Talk about other plants that are similar to gourds.

## Table of Characteristics

| Plant | Color | Size | Shape | Weight |
|---|---|---|---|---|
| gourd | | | | |
| cucumber | | | | |
| squash | | | | |
| pumpkin | | | | |
| watermelon | | | | |

## Processes of Learning

Playing instruments—students will experiment with a variety of (gourd) instruments and play simple melodies on them.

## Suggestions for Related Activities

*Language Arts*: Have the teacher read a section of a native Florida gourd in *Enduring Seeds* by Gary Nabhan (San Francisco: North Point Press, 1989). Let the students talk about the seeds they know and eat. Write the names the students offer into a table of seeds

*Science*: Discuss what seeds are and do. Plant some quick-growing seeds like radish and beans. Continue to measure height of seedlings over a period of a month and record in a table.

*Math*: Count the number of different kinds of gourds and list the characteristics of each kind in a table of observations.

*PE*: Have the class form a marching band and use the gourds to accompany themselves during singing activities.

*Health*: Use some dried seeds of sunflower or pumpkin and nuts to bake a seed/nut bread.

# Listening in the Garden

## Objective
To listen to sounds in the garden.

## Materials
A garden where children can explore and listen to the sounds.
Chart paper
Marker

## Procedure
1. Have the children explore the garden for five to ten minutes and listen and note sounds they hear. Start with a fist and raise a finger for each sound.
2. Listen for sounds that are natural.
3. Listen for sounds that are made by people.
4. Listen to something noisy or quiet, low or deep, high or squeaky; something you like or do not like; or something near or far. Something that is a signal or a warning.
5. Gather the children back into a group and have each one describe the sounds and locations of where they heard them (birds, squirrels, dragonflies, bees, leaves, wind, etc.).
6. Let the children determine whether the sounds were natural or made by people.
7. As a group, fill out the following table.

## Sounds in the Garden

| Sounds | Natural Sounds | Man-made Sounds | Location |
|--------|----------------|-----------------|----------|
|        |                |                 |          |
|        |                |                 |          |
|        |                |                 |          |
|        |                |                 |          |
|        |                |                 |          |
|        |                |                 |          |

## Concepts
Motion, energy and change, biodiversity
*Language Arts*: Word meaning, word identification, sentence structure, gather, evaluate, and synthesize data
Spoken, written, for learning, enjoyment, persuasion, and the exchange of information

## Processes of Learning
Observing, describing, comparing, communicating, measuring, recording

*Math*: Counting the sounds, using *most* and *fewer*

## Suggestions for Related Activities
*Art*: Draw some of the animals that made the sounds.

## Songs of Nature

### Objectives
1. To practice different rhythms or beats.
2. To use their voices to mimic (make) bird sounds or the wind. (Imitate duck calls or bird calls.)

### Materials
Sticks or percussive sticks (for making beats)
A garden (where students can hear a stream, birds, insects)

### Procedure
1. Practice creating a beat by having the teacher first clap a beat and then have the class mimic it.
2. Practice different rhythms by having the teacher first clap a rhythm then have the class mimic it.
3. Practice using voices as instruments by creating low sounds, high sounds, or sounds that go low to high and high to low.
4. Use different words to form the sound around.
5. Choose different sounds from nature (e.g., tree, pond, creek, bird, fly, insects, bees/yellow jackets).

### Processes of Learning
Singing expressively with appropriate dynamics, phrasing, and interpretation.
Improvising simple rhythmic variations.
Performing on instruments, alone and with others, a varied repertoire of music.
Improvising melodies, variations, and accompaniments.

### Suggestions for Related Activities
*Language Arts*: Read poetry with different rhythms or sing songs with different rhythms.

*Math*: Count the number of different rhythms or beat sessions (e.g., steady sound; one long, two short pattern; one long, three short pattern).

*PE*: Band music, marching band.

*Science*: Physical feeling of length of sounds.

Music: "Listen to and sing along with songs from the CD recording or songbook: "Singing in Our Garden" by the Banana Slug String Band, P.O. Box 2262, Santa Cruz, CA 95063.

# Let's Make Believe

# The Leaf Fairy

## Objective
To look (in the autumn) at leaves in the garden and make a leaf fairy.

## Note to Leader
A little girl followed the path along a woodsy creek to school. On the way, she kept losing her homework, notes to the teacher, or whatever she was supposed to carry. The other children would find them and bring them in. One day, she found a leaf skeleton in the creek. All the leaf had washed away except the lacy pattern of veins. At school, she carefully pasted it on a piece of paper, drew on a face, hands, and feet, and wrote a story about the little fairy that lost her leaf. From that true experience, told by a California teacher, the authors derived the following plan.

## Materials
Leaves from the garden
Scissors
Tape
Colored pencils or crayons

## Procedure
1. Show the children how to pick a leaf or instruct them to pick up only one from the ground. If they pick one from the tree, avoid a terminal leaf because that will change the shape of the tree. They might look for lacy leaf skeletons in shallow water.
2. Have them tape a leaf to a piece of paper. It will be the fairy's body.
3. Draw its face and arms and legs. Finish the picture any way they want to.

Encourage the children to tell a story about the leaf fairy they have just made.

For older children, ask these questions:
1. How long are the leaf stems?
2. Describe the edges of the leaf.
3. How are the veins arranged?

## Concepts
Imaginative play
Form and design
Care of personal property

## Suggestions for Related Activities
*Language Arts*: Describe the leaf fairy so that someone else can tell what it is.
Write a story or poem about the leaf fairy. This can be individual or group.

*Math*: Measure the length of the fairy leaves the children have chosen.

# Playing House and Playing Store

## Objective
To use plants for playhouses, stores, and theaters.

## Note to Leader
These activities are based on the childhood free play of an author and her siblings. Your children will come up with similar games with their own ideas if given time and, perhaps, a suggestion or two.

## Materials
Various combinations of the following:
Large shrubs with branches that arch to the ground but have room to walk or crawl around inside
Trees that drop litter on the ground
Clover and plantain or other large flat leaves
Lilac heart-shaped leaves
Trees with low, swishy branches
Long ornamental grass leaves or sedums with sinews
Playhouse furniture and dolls

## Procedure
Choose the largest shrub for the store. The stock can be totally imaginary or representative (e.g., hollyhock seed heads that look like cheese rounds).
Make leaf money. (See115 the activity "Leaf Money").
Rake leaf litter into blueprint-like outlines of rooms. Arrange playhouse furniture and dolls.
In autumn, pack leaves into the bushes to make crawl-through rooms. (This works particularly well in the shrubbery along a foundation.)
Gently rub mullein leaves on the cheeks of the children to raise a little natural color for rouge.
Improvise stage curtains by pulling low branches together or back.
Make thread of the long fibers from grasses or sedums (e.g., century plant).

Notice that sorrel leaves look like sheeps' heads; therefore, it is called sheep's head sorrel.

This is a soil indicator in that it grows on acid soil, and its presence tells the gardener to add lime (see activities "Playing with Dandelions" and "Play Money").

**Concepts and Processes of Learning**
Development: Creative thinking
Math: Shapes, money
Social interaction

## Hollyhock Dolls

**Objective**

To make dolls from hollyhock blossoms.

**Note to Leader**

Hollyhocks are poisonous to eat. Be sure the children do not put them in their mouths.

**Materials**

Stem with enough flowers for all the children in the group
Enough toothpicks for each person to have one (and a few extra)

**Directions**

1. Pick a flower from the stem.
2. Pick off its petiole (the flower stalk) so there is a round top to the flower thorax.
3. Grasp a flower in one hand.
4. With your other hand, push the toothpick through the center of the flower.
5. Leave about a half-inch of the toothpick extending upward and the other end just even with the edge of the flower petals.
6. Now pick a bud off the stalk. Get one that's as round as possible.
7. Put the bud on the extended toothpick.
8. Now stand the flower on its corolla (ring of petals) with the bud on top.
9. You have a doll! You can play with her as such or pretend she is a fairy.

Now pick a seed head from the stalk. Open it gently and you can pretend it is a round of cheese for her to eat.

**Concepts and Processes of Learning**

*Science*: To be able to identify flower parts. Notice the progression down the stalk from the bud to the flowers to the seed heads.

*Language*: Botanical vocabulary; creative play with the dolls; and naming the colors of the blossoms: red, rose, pink, white.

*Art*: Construction in three dimensions.

*Math*: Measuring and size concept.

Adapted from *Dog Days on the Farm* by Lou Hooker (Fremont, Michigan).

# Leaf Money

## Objective
To make toy money in order to play store.

## Note to Leader
This is a child-created activity, a good reminder to let children's imagination soar.

## Materials
Leaves provided by an American or Canadian eastern or mid-western lawn (in which no weed killer has been used)
Clover
Mullein, plantain, or other large flat leaves

## Procedure
Pick the leaflets from clovers for coins.
According to the children's ages, just call them coins or pennies or decide the larger ones can be quarters, the smaller ones dimes, etc.
Use long wide leaves from plantain or mullein for dollar bills.

As the children find leaves to use, talk about them using their common names.
Use the vocabulary to describe the leaf shapes and to name the parts of the leaves:
petiole, blade, tooth, and lobe.

This is harder: use a large heart-shaped leaf, such a large leaf, a grape leaf, or a hollyhock leaf, to make a coin purse.
Hold it with the stem, or petiole, up. Fold up the point to make the bottom of the purse.
Fold over the two sides and overlap them slightly in the center.
Fold down the stem and poke it in to make the top and close the purse.
Put in the clover leaflets for coins and plantain or mullein leaves for dollar bills.

**Concepts**
*Math*: Relative size of coins
*Language Arts*: Becoming familiar with the vocabulary related to leaf shapes, leaf parts, kinds of money, and directions.

**Processes of Learning**
*Art*: Learning shapes by using them.
*Thinking Skills*: Developing creative imagination.
*Science*: Notice the progression down the stalk from the bud on top to the flower and seed head near the bottom.

## Lilac Leaf Purse

## to hold clover leaflet coins

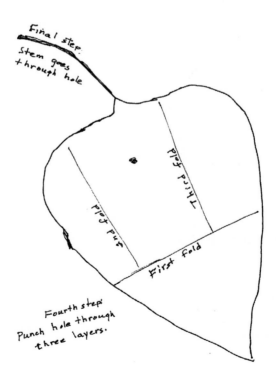

## **Imitating Animals**

**Objective**
To find animals that fly, crawl, walk, jump, and hop in the garden.
To pretend that the children are those animals and show how they
move.

**Note to Leader**
The children may want to get down on the ground to do this. Be sure
it is a sandy or grassy place or tell them to try to do the action while
standing up.

**Procedure**
1. Find a bird or a butterfly or an insect. Pretend you are something
   that flies.
2. Find a centipede or snail or sow bug that crawls. Show how you
   can crawl.
3. Find a rabbit and show how you can hop.
4. Find an earthworm and show how you can wiggle.

**Concepts**
*Science*: Animal behavior.

**Processes of learning**
Observing, communicating, describing through movement

**Suggestions for Related Activities**
*Music*: Clap your hands in time with the way each one moves. Sing
songs about the various animals.

*Art*: Make a finger painting to show how each one goes.

*Language Arts*: Write a poem about things that move. Listen to poems and stories about animals (e. g., "The centipede was happy quite" or "Nice Mr. Rabbit with a Fluffy Tail")

# Moving with the Wind

**Objective**

To act and move like plants and animals in the wind.

**Note to Leader**

This activity is for a breezy day and requires an open space that the children can run across.

**Materials**

Large sheets of tissue paper (one for each child)

**Procedure**

1. Pretend you are a tree or bush or plant in the garden.
2. Show how your stem, trunk, or branches sway in the wind.
3. Pretend you are the clouds and the wind. Show how you can move.
4. Stand on the side of the windward side of the garden. Hold one edge of the paper high with both hands. Follow the paper across the garden.
5. Talk about how it felt to move like the wind.

**Concepts**

*Science*: wind

**Processes of Learning**

*Health*: running, dancing

**Suggestions for Related Activities**

*Language Arts*: Read wind and cloud stories, Native American tales of wind, water, sky, etc. Write a poem about things that move.

*Math*: Count the number of trees and bushes in the vicinity.

*Science*: List the names of some of the flowers and animals in the garden.

*Visual Arts*: Imitate Isadora Duncan's dances of flowing movements in the garden.

*Art*: Make a drawing that shows tree branches moving in the garden.

*Physical Geography*: Figure out which direction the wind is blowing from: north, east, west, south.

*Music*: Clap your hands in time with the way something moves. Imitate the sound of wind as it blows through trees.

# Let's Play a Game

# Finger Play

**Objective**
To enjoy a break from weeding.

**Note to Leader**
Finger plays are pleasant ways to get children's attention.

**Procedure**
Read or recite the play with the motions indicated in parenthesis.
Then have the children do it with you.

> Nice, Mr. Carrot (one thumb up)
> Makes curly hair (twinkle fingers around head)
> His head grows underneath the ground (thumb down)
> His feet in the air (two fingers up)
> And early in the morning
> I jump up from my bed
> And give his feet a great big tug (pull two fingers that are up)
> And up comes his head! (up comes thumb)
>
> (From an old college notebook)

**Concepts**
*Science*: Parts of a carrot
*Development*: Imagination, hand exercise

**Processes of Learning**
*Language*: Following a demonstration, listening, speaking

## <u>Pretending to Be a Plant or an Animal</u>

**Objective**

To increase children's vocabulary and to develop an awareness of the characteristics of plants, animals, and self.

**Materials**

Clipboard and marker (for leader)

**Procedure**

1. Have the children sit in a large circle in the garden.
2. Let the children look around at their surroundings.
3. Get the children to use a single adjective to describe the characteristics of a plant or animal they see (examples: flower—beautiful, fly—pesky, maple tree—tall).
4. Have the children respond to the following questions: If you were a flower, what flower would you be? If you were an animal, insect, bird, place in nature, use an adjective to describe your character.
5. Record your observations.

### Table of Adjectives

| Object Type | Adjective |
|-------------|-----------|
| Flower      |           |
| Fly, insect |           |
| Maple tree  |           |

**Concepts**

Vocabulary
Dramatic Play

**Processes of Learning**
Describing words


**Suggestions for Related Activities**
*Math*: Record how many "personalities" were observed.

*Science*: Record time of day, temperature, and season.

*Art*: Draw some plants or animals in the garden.

# Playing with Dandelions

## Objective
To have fun with weeds.

## Materials
A lawn or meadow with dandelions
Magnifying glass or wire loop (optional)

## Procedure
Blow on seed head. It is said that if all the parachutes fly off, your wish will come true.
Notice that each seed has a parachute.

The flower is really a head of tiny blossoms. When children bring you one, exclaim, "Oh, you brought me a whole bouquet! Thank you." Then show them with a hand lens that there are many tiny flowers in the head.

Pick the longest stems you can find. Loop the small end into the large end and link them to form a chain.

Tuck the small end of each stem into the large end of another and continue to make a pipeline. One little brother irrigated the sandbox in this way!

Use the long stems for straws to drink through.

Notice how the edge of the leaf looks like a lion's teeth? That is why they are called dandelions.

If the dandelions are growing on a clean lawn, pick the leaves and buds to make a salad.

**Concepts**
*Language*: Vocabulary
*Science*: Plant structure, seed dispersal

**Processes of Learning**
Creative thinking

**Suggestions for Related Activities**
*Health*: Outdoor play
Cooking or eating dandelion green salad

## Playing with Shadows

**Objective**
To notice how the shadows change during the day.

**Note to Leader**
To measure the shadow of any garden plant provides an opportunity
to measure and compare distance, contrast height to length of shadow,
and demonstrate the earth's rotation toward the sun in the morning
and away from the sun in the afternoon. People say the sun moves, but
even though the sun moves through space, the shadow is formed by
the earth's rotation as it goes around the sun. A shadow is made when
any object is between a space and the source of light.

It is amazing how fast a shadow lengthens in the late afternoon hours.
For example, a two-foot shrub may cast a shadow of about one foot at
noon, but at four, it may cast a four-foot shadow. The shadow of the
highest point of the plant moves across the lawn at the fastest rate.

**Materials**
Measuring tape
Compass
Gardener's flag markers, stakes, or any object to lay on the ground to
mark a point
Notepad and pencil
Scissors
Lab thermometer (that shows temperature changes quickly)
Roll of twine

**Procedure**
1.  Let's see how the shadow of a plant changes.
2.  Ask the children the following questions:
    What makes shadows?
    When are the shadows longest?

Where is the ground covered by the shadow? Predict where it will be later today.

Is the same part of the garden always in the shade?

What is moving, the sun or the earth?

3.  Let's choose a plant that makes a shadow on a level space and see how it changes while we are here. The plant can be any height. Be sure there is plenty of level open space on the side away from the sun.
4.  Place a flag or stake at the tip of the shadow farthest from the plant that is making the shadow.
5.  After a half hour or longer, return to the shadow.
6.  Place another flag at the part of the shadow that is farthest from the plant now. Repeat at fairly frequent intervals.
7.  Look at the row of flags. Measure the length of the shadow to the flag at each spot.
8.  If the plant is not too tall, measure the height of the plant.
9.  Ask the following questions:
    When is the shadow shorter than the plant, or whatever is casting the shadow?
    When is it longer?
10. Measure the temperature in the shade and in the sun.
11. Discuss that some plants need or grow best in the sun, some need shade part of the time, and some need shade all the time.

Read this piece:

I have a little shadow,
That goes in and out with me,
And what can be the use of him,
Is more than I can see.

—Robert Louis Stevenson
*A Child's Garden of Verses* (1913)

**Processes of Learning**

*Math*: Measuring the shadow, reading a thermometer, comparing lengths

*Language*: Recording data, enjoying poetry

**Suggestions for Related Activities**

*Physical Education*: Play shadow tag by trying to step on someone else's shadow.

*Math*: Spatial concepts

*Art*: Trace someone else's shadow on sand with a stick or on cement with sidewalk chalk.

## Enjoying Garden Poetry

**Objective**
To appreciate outdoor poetry.

**Note to Leader**
Keep a few poems in your pocket to pull out at opportune times when the object of the poem is evident. The Internet has collections of poetry for young children if you search for "poems for young children" or "poetry-archive."

Poetry is a reaction to an experience. Otherwise just a jumble of nonsense will result. One day, the best poem offered by a child was "Foggy woggy, Hit a froggy."

**Materials**
A pocketful of cards of poetry
A notepad and pencil (for the leader)
Chart paper marker

**Procedure**
Summarize the day by having each child name something with one word. Go around again and have the children say the words in rapid succession. They have a poem!
Jot down the words. As soon as possible, rearrange the words to have some semblance of a meter. Put them on a chart so the children can read their own group "poem."
Following is an example of what you might get:

Blue jay, frog
Grass and clover
Pansies bushes roses
Forget-me-nots
In our garden

**Concepts**
Appreciation


**Processes of Learning**
Listening
Composing a poem
Observing, describing, communicating
*Literature:* Instilling a love of poetry, vocabulary
*Music*: Making up a tune for the words

# Let's Enjoy Winter

## **Playing in the Snow**

**Objective**
To enjoy being outdoors in winter.

**Note to Leader**
The garden may seem dormant, but children still want to play in it. Be sure they are dressed warmly and have footwear that will keep their feet dry. Snow angels and tobogganing or just sliding on ice puddles are good for cold days. On warmer days, when the snow is wet, the children can make snowballs.

**Materials**
Snow that is not too deep to walk in
For the snowman:
Some sticks
Pieces of bark (optional)
A carrot
An old hat or cap
For the cave:
Short-handled shovel
Pieces of debris
Small glass jar for a paper weight

**Procedure**
Make snow angels. Every generation learns this folk activity. Tell the children to lie flat on the snow and move their arms up and down, and legs, still on the ground, apart and in. Get up carefully so as not to spoil the design. See the imprint of a winged angel lying on the snow. Usually, one or more already know the activity and can show the others how to do it.

Make snowballs to throw at a target. Throwing snowballs at each other is fun for a short time, but set some rules. Do not throw at the other person's face. Decide a fair distance, depending on the age of the child. Stop the game while it is still fun.

Make a snowman. Roll three large balls. Decide which is the largest. With the help of an older person, set the middle-sized one on it. Set the smallest one on top. Talk about the highest and the lowest. Find and attach broken sticks for arms. Talk about where to attach them and compare the position to the child's own shoulders. Select some small dark objects for buttons—pieces of bark or whatever is handy. Place the buttons. How many did you use?
Put eyes, a nose, and a mouth on the top snowball. Compare the placement to a friend's face. Ask the questions: How far apart are the eyes? Where does the nose go? Use a carrot if one is available. (Optional: find an old hat or broom to complete the project.)

Dig a cave. Dig a cave in a snowdrift (only if the snow is not too deep so that it won't smother the children if they cannot dig themselves out in case of a collapse).

Make a snow fort. Roll snowballs as large as you can. Set the snowballs side by side to make a wall. You might be able to make them two layers high to make a snow fort. Use a piece of old sheet metal, large cardboard, or refrigerator panel to make a roof. An older child may have to help with the roof. Children can use the walls as dividers for snowball fights, or they can play for hours in the snow cave or fort.

Go tobogganing. A refrigerator panel also makes a toboggan. To keep from spinning around, be sure the heaviest weight is on the downhill end. Be sure there is nothing dangerous to bump into at the base of the slope.

Slide on the ice. If a dip in the ground is frozen, slide on the ice. Ask this question: does the ice float on top of or under the water? (Sometimes ice melts on the top, so there are puddles on the top.) On a dried puddle, turn over a piece of ice and look at the design under it. Does this look like a glass castle?

<u>Break off an icicle</u>. What can you do with it? What do you think made it? (It can be sharp.)

<u>Watch the clouds pass.</u> Let's lie on our backs and watch the clouds pass.

<u>Collect some sand</u>. Collect sand and stir some into dry tempera powder of different colors. Then carefully pour some into a clean jar. Keep adding layers of different colors. Close the jar. This makes a pretty paperweight.

<u>Look at rocks</u>. Tell the children to feel which side is warm and which side is cool. Is there ice in a crack? When water turns to ice, it gets bigger and splits the rock! If it isn't too large, roll it toward you so anything under it doesn't run toward your face. What is under it?

<u>Make a weed bouquet.</u> Gather dry plants from the vegetable garden or along the fence row. Make a weed bouquet. With help, make a dry weed mobile.

<u>Look for marks on the bark of the birch trees</u>. There is an Indian legend that a hawk was chasing a little bird. It flew into the birch tree for safety, and if you look carefully, you will see the outline of the little bird.

## Concepts and Processes of Learning
*Health*: outdoor physical activity, appropriate outdoor clothing, physical features (placement of facial features, arms, buttons, etc.)

*Math*: Space relationships, number of buttons, snowballs, size (biggest, smallest, heaviest)

*Science*: cold, frost, friction, changes in matter, weather, insulation, hibernation, microclimates

*Language*: vocabulary, listening to a story

*Art*: designs in nature


## Suggestions for Related Activities
Do the activity "Clouds," page 46.
Do the activity "Interesting Little Stones," page 41.
This is a good time for bark rubbings. Do the activity "Discovering Textures," page 76.

## Gathering Food in Winter

**Objective**
To find something to eat in a winter garden.

**Note to Leader**
Certain vegetables may be planted and harvested in the winter months (e.g., the cabbage family and peas). The following activity is designed for places where the ground may freeze in the winter. Kale is more tender after frost.

**Materials**
Something to cut cabbages or to dig root vegetables (if needed)
(Younger children should not use cabbage knives. Show older children how to cut away from themselves.)
A basket

**Procedure**
In an old vegetable garden, look for kale and corn ears. There might be carrots and other root crops under the snow. Ask if something else has been eating there. For examples, there may be deer or rabbit tracks or perhaps nibbles on vegetables.

In the fall, wrap some apples in long grass and hide them in the tall grass at the edge of the garden. In February or March, ask the children if they remember having done that. Then look for them and find out what happened. They may be perfectly edible and delicious. They were insulated by the grass and snow that covered them and kept from freezing by the warm earth below.

If you live in a hardwood region, you might help the children drive a spigot into a maple tree and hang on a small bucket or plastic bag to collect sap. It takes thirty cups to make one cup of syrup! If you help the child boil it down, do it outdoors because, otherwise, the ceiling gets coated with sticky brown residue from the steam.

Ask where does the rest of the liquid go. Introduce the concept of evaporation.


## Concepts
*Science*: Evaporation, frost, dormancy, insulation, seasons
*Environment*: Survival
*Health*: Nutrition

## Tracks in the Snow

**Objective**
To find tracks in the snow.

**Note to Leader**
In the snow or in muddy spots, the children may find tracks of winter animals (squirrels, birds, rabbits, voles, deer) or a nibbled carrot. Under the snow, the children may discover mouse runs. Perhaps there are grassy nests hidden under the snow. They might even find a shrew, a very tiny and fierce little animal that eats mice and insects.

**Materials**
Tracks in the snow

**Procedure**
Find tracks in the snow.
Ask the following questions:
What do you think made them?
Which way was it going?
Was it going fast or slow? Why do you think so?
Was it running, hopping, walking?
Why do you think so?
Why was it here?
Where do you think it was going?
Do you think something scared it? Why do you think so?

They might find deer tracks or nibbled places on carrots or the bark of trees.

Suggest to the children that they make their own tracks in the snow. Follow them back. Try walking backward to fool other people into thinking you went the other way. Make a path for other children to follow. Line up, shuffle your feet, and make a path.
Make a big pie in the snow and play tag staying on the paths.

Read the poem about walking in the snow:

Everything has a song.
Everything needs to sing
Even the snow when I scrunch along
Squeaks like anything.

—Dorothy Aldis
*Very Young Verses*

**Concepts**
*Science*: Observation, inference
*Environment*: Survival

## <u>Watching Winter Birds</u>

**Objectives**
To identify some common winter birds
To learn what they eat and why they are sometimes in flocks.
To learn to look for bird features and actions that help identify the birds.

**Note to Leader**
It is easier to see the birds after the leaves have fallen. The birds will be finding seeds, insects, larvae, and insect eggs. The shape of their bills will tell you if they eat seeds or insects. Seed eaters have short, thick beaks; insect eaters have long, thin beaks. Woodpeckers and canaries fly in scallops, dipping and rising with extra wing thrusts.

In flocks, there are more eyes to watch for danger. For each bird, the chance of being eaten by a hawk is less than with one bird being alone. They face the same way to keep their feathers flat. That way, they are well insulated (Gary Bogue, *Contra Costa Times*).

In some places on hawk flyways, there are more hawks in winter than in summer. This is especially true along the Pacific Coast, in Minnesota, and in Pennsylvania.

If you use bird pictures, be sure they are local birds. Most bird pictures for elementary children are of eastern birds. For example, blue jays and hummingbirds are different in the West.

**Materials**
To make a feeder:
> An old sock without holes
> String
> Thistle seed

A pine cone
Peanut butter
Mixed birdseed

String
Pictures with names of local birds
Close-up pictures of beaks (if available)

**Procedure**
Watch the birds flying over. Talk about what they are doing, where they might be going. Watch the wings. Are they long? Do the front edges fly straight, or do they extend back? Describe the pattern of the bird's flight (straight, scalloped, in flocks, or alone).

Ask these questions: Compared to other birds, do they fly fast or slow? Are they high in the sky or low near the bushes?

Look for birds on a wire. Why do you think they are in flocks? Why do they face the same way?

Through the window, watch the birds in the yard. Perhaps you can name some of the kinds. If they are eating, what are they eating?

Note: They will be finding seeds, insects, larvae, and insect eggs. The shape of their bill will tell you if they eat seeds or insects.

Make a bird feeder. Fill a sock with thistle seed from a store. Tie the top end shut. With a string, hang it to a branch or clothesline.

Take a large pinecone and spread it with chunky peanut butter. Then roll it in birdseed. Tie a string to the broad end and hang it where you can watch it. You may need an adult to reach high enough.

Put out seeds, nuts, and suet for the birds. Go to the local birdseed store for ideas of what local birds eat and how the seed should be placed for them.

**Concepts**
Animal identification
Animal behavior
Seasons
Habitat

**Suggestions for Related Activities**
*Art*: Making a feeder.

*Physical Education*: Imitate birds' wings or back, flying fast and slowly, looking for seeds and insects.

*Language Arts*: Describe the birds' characteristics. Talk about the birds' behavior.

Indoors, make a Venn diagram (two overlapping circles) comparing birds and people

## <u>Looking Closely at Snowflakes</u>

**Objective**
To discover the patterns of water crystals.

**Note to Leader**
Do this activity on a day when the weather is mild and large flakes are drifting down.

**Materials**
A hand lens for each child (optional)

For the follow-up activity:
> Squares of paper about 8″ × 8″ or 6″ × 6″
> Scissors for each child
> String
> Scotch tape
> Folded 8″ × 11″ paper (one sheet for each child)

**Procedure**
Tell the children: Let's catch a snowflake on our mittens! Look at it closely with a magnifying glass, if it is available.

Ask the following questions:
How many sides or points does it have?
Look at more snowflakes. Are any two alike?
How many points do the other snowflakes have?
What happens when the snowflake melts?
Can you catch a snowflake on your tongue?

Follow up indoors:
Afterward, fold a square of paper in half then fold it again into thirds. Open the paper up. If you did it right, there will be six triangles, each with a point in the center of the paper. Fold it again. Take a scissors and cut little snips out of the edges and out of the folds. Open it

up again. If a lot of children do this, they can put the flakes on the windows with masking tape or string them together on a chain. Each child can paste one on a folded sheet of colored paper to make a greeting card.

**Concepts**
*Science*: Crystals

**Processes of Learning**
*Art*: Cutting, pasting, centering, folding (with help)
*Math*: Counting sides, points, and triangles
*Shapes*: Folded square yields six triangles!

Using a hand lens
Following oral directions
Folding
Using a scissors

## Trees and Twigs

**Objective**
To look closely at branches and find the signs of last year's life and the coming spring's growth

**Note to Leader**
The following activity for the dormant season holds interest for adults, but it capitalizes on young children's interest in small things. Keep the time short, and do this when there is not a cold wind. At this age, botanical vocabulary is not needed.

On northern white oaks, the old leaves hang on until the buds swell for the coming year. Then a corky layer pushes off the old leaf. People are like that too. It is useless to pick at people, but if we warm them up with praise and love, they will grow nicely. This is a life lesson learned from an aged Pottawatomie Indian.

**Materials**
None are needed, but if it is not too cold, hand lenses help focus attention.

**Procedure**
Ask the children to pull down and forward a small woody branch. Look for the leaf scars. Find out if they grow opposite each other or alternate on all sides of the branch.
Explain that is where last year's leaf was. Where is the bud for next year?

Examine a bud for next year's leaf. Decide if it is white or red, wooly or smooth, sticking out from the twig or pressed against it. Compare the bud at the end of the twig with the ones at the side. How many are at the end?

Describe the leaf scar. Is it shaped like a valentine? Like a monkey face? Is it round?
Find the openings where the sap flowed to feed the leaves.

How would you describe the bark? Is it smooth, furrowed, scaly, round, bumpy, or rough? What else might feel this way?

Carefully break a box elder (maple) twig and look at the pith in the center. Try to push it out with a small straight twig. Native Americans used these as "plunger" sticks to make syringes.

## Concepts
*Botany*: External woody stem structure, internal stem structure, sap flow, deciduousness, plant growth structures, leaf buds

*Earth Science*: Seasons

*Art*: Attention to detail

## Processes of Learning
Observing. comparing, describing

## Suggestions for Related Activities
*Language*: Vocabulary

*Science*: Predict, observe, determine cause and effect, hypothesize, compare

*Social Studies*: Native uses of plants

*Math*: Measure temperature, length of twigs, circumference of twig, distance between leaf scars

Student_____

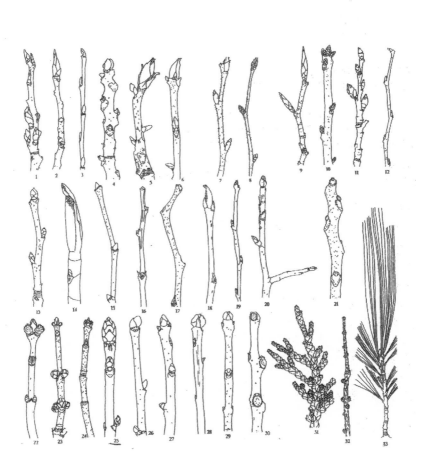

# Appendix

## Appendix A.a

Common Core Standards in English Language Arts

| Things to do | Let's Explore | | | | Let's | | | |
|---|---|---|---|---|---|---|---|---|
| | Home of Animals | Pond Life | Insects Flying on Gossamer | Spider Webs | Will It Rain Soon? | The Garden Air | Interesting Little Stones | Playing with Dirt |
| **Language** | | | | | | | | |
| Vocabulary | • | • | • | • | • | • | • | • |
| Grammar, usage | • | • | • | • | • | | • | • |
| Comprehension | • | • | • | • | • | • | • | • |
| **Presentation of:** | | | | | | | | |
| Knowledge, ideas | • | • | • | • | • | • | • | • |
| Ability to decribe | • | • | • | • | • | • | • | • |
| Speak, express thoughts feelings and ideas | • | • | • | • | • | • | • | • |
| Combine Drawing, dictating and writing | | | • | • | | | • | |
| **Reading Readiness** | | | | | | | | |
| Key ideas and details | • | • | • | • | • | • | • | • |
| Craft and structure (words, author, illustrator, types of books, beginning, end, etc.) | | | • | | • | | | |
| Integration of knowledge and ideas | • | • | • | • | • | • | • | • |
| Reading with purpose | • | • | | | | | | |
| Print concepts (punct. Etc) | | | | | | | | • |
| Phonemes (sound parts) | | | | | | | | |
| **Writing** | | | | | | | | |
| Using a combination of drawing, dictating, writing | | • | • | • | • | | • | • |
| Revising and editing | | | | | | | | • |
| **Speaking and Listening** | | | | | | | | |
| Converse | • | • | • | • | • | • | • | • |
| Describe oral presentation | • | | • | • | • | | • | • |
| Ask and answer questions | • | | • | • | • | • | • | • |
| Tell complete story | • | • | • | • | • | • | • | • |
| Use complete sentences | • | • | • | • | • | • | • | • |
| **Reading** | | | | | | | | |
| Key ideas and deteails | • | • | • | • | | | | • |
| Integration of knowledge and ideas | | • | | • | • | • | • | • |
| Reading with purpose | • | • | | | | | | • |
| to enjoy poetry | | | | | • | | | |
| Print concepts (punct. Etc) | • | • | | | • | • | | • |

| Observe | | | | | | Let's Make Something | | | | | | | | Let's Measure | | | |
|---|---|---|---|---|---|---|---|---|---|---|---|---|---|---|---|---|---|
| Clouds | Behaviour of Living Things | Biodiversity | Effects of Wind | Bird Watching | The Garden at Night | Using Plants as Art Tools | Falling Leaves and Bits of Bark | Preparing Lunch | Seed Design | Drawing Shadows | Making a Collage | Discovering Textures | Arranging Bouquets | Comparing Plants | Shapes | Nature's Geometry | How Many and How Big |
| ● | ● | ● | ● | ● | ● | ● | ● | ● | ● | ● | ● | ● | ● | ● | ● | ● | ● |
| ● | ● | ● | ● | ● | ● | ● | ● | ● | ● | ● | ● | ● | ● | ● | ● | ● | ● |
| ● | ● | ● | ● | ● | ● | ● | ● | ● | ● | ● | ● | ● | ● | ● | ● | ● | ● |
|  |  |  |  |  |  |  |  |  |  |  |  |  |  |  |  |  |  |
| ● | ● | ● | ● | ● | ● | ● | ● | ● | ● | ● | ● | ● | ● | ● | ● | ● | ● |
| ● | ● | ● | ● | ● | ● | ● | ● | ● | ● | ● | ● | ● | ● | ● | ● | ● | ● |
| ● | ● | ● | ● | ● | ● | ● | ● | ● | ● | ● | ● | ● | ● | ● | ● | ● | ● |
| ● | ● | ● | ● | ● | ● | ● | ● | ● | ● | ● |  |  |  | ● | ● | ● | ● |
|  |  |  |  |  |  |  |  |  |  |  |  |  |  |  |  |  |  |
| ● | ● | ● | ● | ● | ● | ● |  | ● | ● | ● | ● | ● | ● | ● | ● | ● | ● |
|  |  | ● |  |  |  |  |  |  | ● |  | ● |  | ● |  |  |  |  |
|  |  | ● |  |  |  |  |  | ● | ● | ● |  |  |  | ● |  |  |  |
|  |  |  |  |  |  |  |  |  |  |  |  |  |  |  |  |  |  |
|  |  |  |  |  |  |  |  |  |  |  |  |  |  |  |  |  |  |
|  | ● | ● | ● | ● |  | ● |  | ● | ● | ● | ● | ● | ● | ● |  | ● | ● |
|  |  |  |  |  |  |  |  |  |  |  | ● |  |  |  |  |  |  |
|  |  |  |  |  |  |  |  |  |  |  |  |  |  |  |  |  |  |
| ● | ● | ● | ● | ● | ● | ● | ● | ● | ● | ● | ● | ● | ● | ● | ● | ● | ● |
| ● | ● | ● | ● | ● | ● |  | ● | ● | ● | ● | ● | ● | ● | ● | ● | ● | ● |
| ● | ● | ● | ● | ● | ● | ● | ● | ● | ● | ● |  |  |  | ● | ● | ● | ● |
| ● | ● | ● | ● | ● | ● |  |  | ● | ● |  |  |  | ● |  |  |  | ● |
| ● | ● | ● | ● | ● | ● | ● | ● | ● | ● | ● | ● | ● | ● | ● | ● | ● | ● |
|  |  |  |  |  |  |  |  |  |  |  |  |  |  |  |  |  |  |
| ● | ● | ● | ● | ● | ● |  | ● |  | ● | ● | ● | ● | ● | ● | ● | ● | ● |
| ● | ● | ● | ● | ● | ● |  |  | ● | ● | ● | ● | ● | ● | ● | ● | ● | ● |
|  |  | ● |  |  |  |  |  | ● | ● |  |  |  |  | ● |  |  |  |
|  |  |  |  | ● |  |  |  |  |  |  |  |  |  |  |  |  |  |
|  |  | ● |  |  |  |  |  |  | ● | ● |  |  |  | ● |  |  |  |

| Appendix A.b<br><br>Common Core Standards in English Language Arts | Things to do | Let's Make Music | | | | | Let's Make | | |
|---|---|---|---|---|---|---|---|---|---|
| | | The Food Chain Song | Nature's Band | Musical Gourds | Listening in the Garden | Songs of Nature | The Leaf Fairy | Playing House and Playing Store | Hollyhock Dolls |
| **Language** | | | | | | | | | |
| Vocabulary | | • | • | • | • | • | • | • | • |
| Grammar, usage | | • | • | • | • | • | • | • | • |
| Comprehension | | • | • | • | • | • | • | • | • |
| **Presentation of:** | | | | | | | | | |
| Knowledge, ideas | | • | • | • | • | • | • | • | • |
| Ability to decribe | | • | • | • | • | • | • | • | • |
| Speak, express thoughts feelings and ideas | | • | • | • | • | • | • | • | • |
| Combine Drawing, dictating and writing | | | | | | | • | | |
| **Reading Readiness** | | | | | | | | | |
| Key ideas and details | | • | • | • | • | • | • | • | • |
| Craft and structure (words, author, illustrator, types of books, beginning, end, etc.) | | | | | | | | | |
| Integration of knowledge and ideas | | • | | • | • | | • | • | |
| Reading with purpose | | | | | | | | | |
| Print concepts (punct. Etc) | | | • | | • | | | | |
| Phonemes (sound parts) | | • | | | • | • | | | |
| **Writing** | | | | | | | | | |
| Using a combination of drawing, dictating, writing | | • | • | • | • | | • | | • |
| Revising and editing | | | | | | | | | |
| **Speaking and Listening** | | | | | | | | | |
| Converse | | | | | • | • | • | • | • |
| Describe oral presentation | | X | • | • | • | • | • | • | • |
| Ask and answer questions | | • | • | • | • | • | • | • | • |
| Tell complete story | | • | • | | • | | • | • | • |
| Use complete sentences | | • | • | • | • | • | • | • | • |
| **Reading** | | | | | | | | | |
| Key ideas and deteails | | | | • | | | | | |
| Integration of knowledge and ideas | | • | | • | • | • | • | • | • |
| Reading with purpose | | | | • | | • | | | |
| to enjoy poetry | | • | | | | | | | |
| Print concepts (punct. Etc) | | | | • | | • | | | |

| Believe | | | Let's Play a Game | | | | | Let's Enjoy Winter | | | | | |
| --- | --- | --- | --- | --- | --- | --- | --- | --- | --- | --- | --- | --- | --- |
| Leaf Money | Imitating Animals | Moving with the Wind | Finger Play | Pretending to be a Plant or Animal | Playing with Dandelions | Playing with Shadows | Enjoying Garden Poetry | Playing in the Snow | Gathering Food in the Winter | Tracks in the Snow | Watching Winter Birds | Looking Closely at Ice and Snow | Trees and Twigs |
| ● | ● | ● | ● | ● | ● | ● | ● | ● | ● | ● | ● | ● | ● |
| ● | ● | ● | ● | ● | ● | ● | ● | ● | ● | ● | ● | ● | ● |
| ● | ● | ● | ● | ● | ● | ● | ● | ● | ● | ● | ● | ● | ● |
|  |  |  |  |  |  |  |  |  |  |  |  |  |  |
| ● | ● | ● | ● | ● | ● | ● | ● | ● | ● | ● | ● | ● | ● |
| ● | ● | ● | ● | ● | ● | ● | ● | ● | ● | ● | ● | ● | ● |
| ● |  | ● | ● |  | ● | ● |  | ● |  | ● | ● | ● | ● |
|  |  |  |  | ● |  | ● | ● |  |  |  |  | ● |  |
|  |  |  |  |  |  |  |  |  |  |  |  |  |  |
| ● | ● | ● | ● | ● | ● | ● | ● | ● | ● | ● | ● | ● | ● |
|  |  |  |  |  |  |  |  |  |  |  |  |  |  |
| ● | ● | ● | ● | ● | ● | ● | ● | ● | ● | ● | ● | ● | ● |
|  |  |  | ● |  |  |  |  |  |  |  |  |  |  |
|  |  |  |  |  |  |  | ● |  |  |  |  |  |  |
|  |  |  |  |  |  |  |  |  |  |  |  |  |  |
|  |  |  |  |  |  |  |  |  |  |  | ● |  |  |
|  |  |  |  |  |  |  |  |  |  |  |  |  |  |
|  |  |  |  |  |  |  | ● |  |  |  |  |  |  |
|  |  |  |  |  |  |  |  |  |  |  |  |  |  |
| ● | ● |  | ● | ● | ● | ● | ● | ● | ● | ● |  | ● | ● |
| ● | ● | ● | ● | ● | ● | ● | ● | ● | ● | ● | ● | ● | ● |
| ● | ● |  | ● | ● | ● | ● | ● | ● | ● | ● | ● | ● | ● |
|  |  |  |  | ● | ● | ● | ● | ● |  | ● |  |  |  |
| ● | ● | ● | ● | ● | ● | ● | ● | ● | ● | ● | ● | ● | ● |
|  |  |  |  |  |  |  |  |  |  |  |  |  |  |
|  |  |  |  |  |  |  |  |  |  |  |  |  |  |
| ● | ● | ● | ● | ● | ● | ● | ● | ● | ● | ● | ● |  |  |
|  |  |  |  |  |  |  |  |  |  |  |  |  |  |
|  |  |  |  |  |  |  | ● |  |  |  |  |  |  |
|  |  |  |  | ● |  |  |  |  |  |  |  |  |  |

| | Things to do | Let's Explore | | | | Let's | | |
|---|---|---|---|---|---|---|---|---|
| Common Core Standards in Mathematics | | Home of Animals | Pond Life | Insects Flying on Gossamer | Spider Webs | Will It Rain Soon? | The Garden Air | Interesting Little Stones |
| **Counting and Cardinal Numbers** | | | | | | | | |
| Number names | | | • | | • | • | | • |
| Counting | | | • | | • | • | | |
| Comparing numbers | | | | • | | • | | |
| Problems | | • | • | • | | | | • |
| Groups | | | • | • | | | | • |
| | | | | | | | | |
| **Operations and Algebraic Thinking** | | | | | | | | |
| Counting | | | • | • | • | • | | |
| | | | | | | | | |
| **Number and Operations** | | | | | | | | |
| Counting | | | • | • | • | • | | |
| Add and subtract | | | • | | | • | | |
| | | | | | | | | |
| **Measurement and Data** | | | | | | | | |
| Classifying | | | • | • | | | | • |
| Lengths | | | • | | | | | • |
| Time and Money | | | • | | | | • | |
| Estimation | | | • | | | | | • |
| Data | | | • | • | • | • | | • |
| | | | | | | | | |
| **Geometry** | | | | | | | | |
| Shapes | | • | | • | • | • | | • |

| Observe | | | | | | | Let's Make Something | | | | | | | | Let's Measure | | | |
|---|---|---|---|---|---|---|---|---|---|---|---|---|---|---|---|---|---|---|
| Playing with Dirt | Clouds | Behaviour of Living Things | Biodiversity | Effects of Wind | Bird Watching | The Garden at Night | Using Plants as Art Tools | Falling Leaves and Bits of Bark | Preparing Lunch | Seed Design | Drawing Shadows | Making a Collage | Discovering Textures | Arranging Bouquets | Comparing Plants | Shapes | Nature's Geometry | How Many and How Big |
|  |  |  | • |  | • |  |  |  | • | • | • | • | • | • | • |  |  | • |
|  |  |  | • |  | • |  |  |  | • | • |  |  | • | • | • |  |  | • |
|  |  |  |  | • |  | • |  |  |  | • | • |  |  | • | • |  |  | • |
| • |  | • |  |  | • |  |  |  |  | • |  |  | • | • | • | • |  | • |
|  |  |  |  |  |  |  |  |  |  |  | • |  |  |  |  |  |  | • |
|  |  |  |  |  |  |  |  |  |  |  |  |  |  |  |  |  |  |  |
|  |  |  | • |  | • |  |  |  | • |  |  |  |  |  | • |  |  | • |
|  |  |  |  |  |  |  |  |  |  |  |  |  |  |  |  |  |  |  |
| • |  |  |  |  | • |  |  |  | • |  |  |  | • | • | • |  |  | • |
| • |  |  |  |  |  |  |  |  |  | • |  | • |  |  | • |  |  |  |
|  |  |  |  |  |  |  |  |  |  |  |  |  |  |  |  |  |  |  |
| • |  | • | • | • | • | • | • | • | • | • | • | • | • | • | • | • | • | • |
| • |  |  |  |  | • |  | • |  |  | • | • | • |  | • | • |  |  | • |
|  |  | • |  | • | • |  | • |  |  |  |  |  |  |  |  |  |  |  |
| • |  | • |  | • | • |  |  |  |  |  |  |  | • |  | • | • | • |  |
| • |  | • |  | • | • |  |  | • | • | • | • | • | • | • | • | • | • | • |
|  |  |  |  |  |  |  |  |  |  |  |  |  |  |  |  |  |  |  |
| • | • | • | • | • | • | • | • | • | • | • | • | • | • | • | • | • | • | • |

| Appendix B.b<br><br>Common Core Standards in Mathematics | Things to do | Let's Make Music | | | | | Let's Make | | |
|---|---|---|---|---|---|---|---|---|---|
| | | The Food Chain Song | Nature's Band | Musical Gourds | Listening in the Garden | Songs of Nature | The Leaf Fairy | Playing House and Playing Store | Hollyhock Dolls |
| **Counting and Cardinal Numbers** | | | | | | | | | |
| Number names | | | | • | | | | • | |
| Counting | | • | • | • | • | • | • | | |
| Comparing numbers | | | • | • | | | | | |
| Problems | | • | | • | | • | | • | |
| Groups | | | | | | | | | |
| | | | | | | | | | |
| **Operations and Algebraic Thinking** | | | | | | | | | |
| Counting | | | | • | | | | | |
| | | | | | | | | | |
| **Number and Operations** | | | | | | | | | |
| Counting | | | | | | | | • | |
| Add and subtract | | | | | | | | • | |
| | | | | | | | | | |
| **Measurement and Data** | | | | | | | | | |
| Classifying | | • | • | • | • | • | • | • | • |
| Lengths | | | • | • | | | • | • | • |
| Time and Money | | | | | | | | • | |
| Estimation | | | | | | | | • | • |
| Data | | • | • | • | • | | | | • |
| | | | | | | | | | |
| **Geometry** | | | | | | | | | |
| Shapes | | | • | • | | | • | • | • |

| Believe | | | Let's Play a Game | | | | | Let's Enjoy Winter | | | | | |
|---|---|---|---|---|---|---|---|---|---|---|---|---|---|
| Leaf Money | Imitating Animals | Moving with the Wind | Finger Play | Pretending to be a Plant or Animal | Playing with Dandelions | Playing with Shadows | Enjoying Garden Poetry | Playing in the Snow | Gathering Food in the Winter | Tracks in the Snow | Watching Winter Birds | Looking Closely at Ice and Snow | Trees and Twigs |
| • | | | • | • | | • | | | | | • | • | |
| • | | • | | | | | | • | • | | • | • | • |
| | | | | | • | | • | • | | | • | | |
| • | • | • | | | • | | • | | | • | • | • | |
| • | | | | | | | | | | | • | | |
| | | | | | | | | | | | | | |
| | | | | | | | | | | | | | |
| | | | | | | | | | | | | • | |
| | | | | | | | | | | | | | |
| • | | | | | | | | | | | | • | |
| | | | | | | | | | | | | | |
| | | | | | | | | | | | | | |
| • | • | • | | | • | • | | • | • | | | • | |
| • | | | | | | • | • | | | | • | | • |
| • | | | | | | • | | | | • | | | • |
| • | | | | | | | | • | • | | • | | |
| | | | | | • | • | • | • | • | | | | • |
| | | | | | | | | | | | | | |
| | | | | | | | | | | | | | |
| • | • | • | • | • | • | • | • | • | • | • | • | • | • |

| Appendix C.1.a<br><br>Next Generation Science Standards K-2<br><br>**Things to do** | Let's Explore | | | | Let's | | |
|---|---|---|---|---|---|---|---|
| | Home of Animals | Pond Life | Insects Flying on Gossamer | Spider Webs | Will It Rain Soon? | The Garden Air | Interesting Little Stones |
| **Earth Space Science Progression** | | | | | | | |
| 1. ESS1.A, ESS1.B Universe and Earth and Solar system. Patterns of movement of sub, moon, stars, observed, described, and predicted | | | | | | | |
| 2. ESS2.A Earth materials and systems Wind and water change the land shape | | • | | | | | |
| 3. ESS2.C Roles of water in Earth's surface processes. | | | | | • | | • |
| 4. Environment ESS2.D Weather and climate rain, snow, rain, temperature, recording weather patterns | • | • | • | • | • | | |
| 5. ESS3.A Natural Resources Living things need water, air, land resources | | | | | | | |
| **Life Science Progression** | | | | | | | |
| 1. LSI.A Structure and Function | • | • | • | • | | | |
| 2. LSI.B Growth and Development | | • | | | | | |
| 3. LSI.C Organization for matter and energy flow in organisms. | | | | | | | |
|    Animals obtain food from plants or other animals | | • | • | • | | | |
|    Plants need water and light | | • | • | | | | |
| 4. LSI.D Information Processing Organisms sense and communicate info | • | • | • | • | | | |
| 5. LS2.A and LSI.A Interdependent relationships in ecosystems | • | • | • | • | | | |
| 6. LS2.B , LSI.C and ESS3.A Cycles of matter and energy transfer | • | • | • | • | | | |
| 7. LS4.C Adaptation Living thing's survival needs | • | • | • | • | | | |
| 8. LS4.D Biodiversity A range of different organisms live in different places | • | • | • | • | • | | |
| **Physical Science Progression** | | | | | | | |
| 1. PSI.A Structure of Matter | • | | | | | | • |
| 2. PSI.B Chemical Reactions, heating and cooling | | | | | | | |
| 3. PS2.A, PS2.B Forces and Motion, Types of interactions | | • | • | | | • | |
| 4. PS3.B, PS3.D Conservation of energy and energy transfer | | • | | | | | |
| 5. PS3.C Energy and forces relationship, pushes and pulls | | | | | | • | |
| 6. PS3.D Energy in chemical processes and everyday life, sunlight | • | • | | | | | |
| 7. PS4.A Wave properties | | • | • | | | • | • |

| | Observe | | | | | | | Let's Make Something | | | | | | | | Let's Measure | | | |
|---|---|---|---|---|---|---|---|---|---|---|---|---|---|---|---|---|---|---|---|
| | Playing with Dirt | Clouds | Behaviour of Living Things | Biodiversity | Effects of Wind | Bird Watching | The Garden at Night | Using Plants as Art Tools | Falling Leaves and Bits of Bark | Preparing Lunch | Seed Design | Drawing Shadows | Making a Collage | Discovering Textures | Arranging Bouquets | Comparing Plants | Shapes | Nature's Geometry | How Many and How Big |
| | | | | | | | • | | | | | • | | | | | | | |
| | • | | | | • | | | | | | | | • | | | | | | |
| | • | | | | • | | | | | | | | | | | | | | |
| | | | • | | | • | • | | • | • | | | | | | | | • | • |
| | | | | | | • | | | | • | | | | | | • | | | • |
| | | | • | • | • | • | | • | • | • | • | • | | • | • | • | | • | • |
| | | | • | • | | | | | | | • | | | | | | | | |
| | | | | | | | | | | | | | | | | | | | |
| | | | • | • | | | | | • | | | | | | | | | | |
| | | | • | • | • | • | | | • | | • | | | • | | • | | | • |
| | | | • | | • | | • | | | | | | | | | | • | | |
| | | | • | • | | | | • | | | | | | | | | | | |
| | | | • | • | • | | | | | | | | | | • | | | | |
| | | | • | • | • | • | | | • | • | | | | | • | • | | | |
| | | | • | • | | • | • | | • | • | • | • | • | • | • | • | • | • | • |
| | • | • | | | • | | | | | | | | | • | | | | | |
| | | | | | | | | | | | | | | | | | | | |
| | • | • | | | • | • | | • | | | | | • | | | | | | |
| | • | | | | • | | | | | | | | | | | | | | |
| | | | • | | • | | | • | | | | | | | | | | | |
| | | | | | | | | • | | | | | | | | | | | |
| | | • | | | • | • | • | | • | | | • | | | | | | • | |

| Appendix C.1.b  Next Generation Science Standards K-2 | Things to do | Let's Make Music | | | | | Let's Make | | |
|---|---|---|---|---|---|---|---|---|---|
| | | The Food Chain Song | Nature's Band | Musical Gourds | Listening in the Garden | Songs of Nature | The Leaf Fairy | Playing House and Playing Store | Hollyhock Dolls |
| **Earth Space Science Progression** | | | | | | | | | |
| 1. ESS1.A, ESS1.B Universe and Earth and Solar system. Patterns of movement of sub, moon, stars, observed, described, and predicted | | • | | | | | | | |
| 2. ESS2.A Earth materials and systems Wind and water change the land shape | | | | | | | | | |
| 3. ESS2.C Roles of water in Earth's surface processes. | | | | | | | | | |
| 4. Environment ESS2.D Weather and climate rain, snow, rain, temperature, recording weather patterns | | • | | | | | | | |
| 5. ESS3.A Natural Resources Living things need water, air, land resources | | | | | | | | | |
| **Life Science Progression** | | | | | | | | | |
| 1. LSI.A Structure and Function | | • | • | • | | | • | • | • |
| 2. LSI.B Growth and Development | | | | • | | | | | |
| 3. LSI.C Organization for matter and energy flow in organisms. | | | | | | | | | |
| Animals obtain food from plants or other animals | | • | | • | | | | | |
| Plants need water and light | | • | | • | | | | | |
| 4. LSI.D Information Processing Organisms sense and communicate info | | | | | • | • | | | |
| 5. LS2.A and LSI.A Interdependent relationships in ecosystems | | | | | | | | | |
| 6. LS2.B , LSI.C and ESS3.A Cycles of matter and energy transfer | | • | | | | | | | |
| 7. LS4.C Adaptation Living thing's survival needs | | | | | | | | | |
| 8. LS4.D Biodiversity A range of different organisms live in different places | | • | • | • | • | • | | • | |
| **Physical Science Progression** | | | | | | | | | |
| 1. PSI.A Structure of Matter | | | | | | | | | |
| 2. PSI.B Chemical Reactions, heating and cooling | | | | | | | | | |
| 3. PS2.A, PS2.B Forces and Motion, Types of interactions | | | • | | • | | | | |
| 4. PS3.B, PS3.D Conservation of energy and energy transfer | | | | | | | | | |
| 5. PS3.C Energy and forces relationship, pushes and pulls | | | • | | | | | | |
| 6. PS3.D Energy in chemical processes and everyday life, sunlight | | | | | | | | | |
| 7. PS4.A Wave properties | | • | • | • | • | • | | | |

| Believe | | | Let's Play a Game | | | | | Let's Enjoy Winter | | | | | |
| --- | --- | --- | --- | --- | --- | --- | --- | --- | --- | --- | --- | --- | --- |
| Leaf Money | Imitating Animals | Moving with the Wind | Finger Play | Pretending to be a Plant or Animal | Playing with Dandelions | Playing with Shadows | Enjoying Garden Poetry | Playing in the Snow | Gathering Food in the Winter | Tracks in the Snow | Watching Winter Birds | Looking Closely at Ice and Snow | Trees and Twigs |
|  |  |  |  |  |  |  |  |  |  |  |  |  |  |
|  |  |  |  |  |  | • |  |  |  |  |  |  |  |
|  |  |  |  |  |  |  |  |  |  |  |  |  |  |
|  |  |  |  | • |  | • |  | • | • | • |  | • | • |
|  |  |  |  |  |  |  |  |  |  |  |  |  | • |
| • | • | • | • | • | • |  |  | • | • | • | • |  | • |
|  |  |  |  |  |  |  |  |  |  |  |  |  |  |
|  |  |  |  |  |  |  |  |  |  |  |  |  |  |
|  |  |  |  |  |  |  |  | • |  |  |  |  | • |
|  |  |  |  |  |  |  |  |  |  |  | • |  |  |
|  |  |  |  |  |  |  |  |  |  |  |  |  |  |
|  |  |  |  |  | • |  |  |  |  |  | • |  | • |
|  | • | • |  | • |  |  | • |  | • | • | • |  |  |
|  |  |  |  |  |  |  |  |  |  |  |  |  |  |
|  |  |  |  |  |  |  |  | • |  |  |  |  |  |
|  |  |  |  |  |  |  |  | • |  |  |  | • |  |
|  |  |  |  |  |  |  |  | • | • |  | • |  |  |
|  |  |  |  |  |  |  |  |  |  |  | • |  |  |
|  |  |  |  |  |  |  |  |  |  |  |  |  |  |
|  |  |  |  |  |  |  |  | • | • | • |  |  |  |
|  |  |  |  |  |  |  |  | • |  | • |  |  | • |
|  |  | • |  |  |  |  | • |  |  | • |  |  |  |

155

| Appendix D.1.a<br><br>NAEYC Accreditation Criteria for Curriculum | Things to do | Let's Explore | | | | Let's | | | |
|---|---|---|---|---|---|---|---|---|---|
| | | Home of Animals | Pond Life | Insects Flying on Gossamer | Spider Webs | Will It Rain Soon? | The Garden Air | Interesting Little Stones | Playing with Dirt |
| **Children have opportunities to**<br>**2.B Social-Emotional Development** | | | • | | • | • | • | • | • |
| 1. Relate to others | | • | • | • | | | • | • | |
| 2. Express Feelings | | • | | • | • | • | • | | |
| 3. Learn Skills | | | | | | | | | • |
| 4. Develop confidence | | | | • | | | | | |
| 5. Enter social groups | | | | | | | | • | |
| 6. Copperate | | | | | | | | • | • |
| 7. Develop Empathy | | | | | | | | | |
| **2.C Physical Development** | | | | | | | | | |
| 1. move freely | | • | • | • | | | | • | • |
| 2. use fingers and hands | | | | | | | | | • |
| 3. develop fine motor | | | | | | | | • | |
| 4. Have large motor experiences | | • | • | • | | | | • | • |
| **2.D Language Development** | | | | | | | | | |
| 2.D.01Align with learning environment | | • | | • | • | • | • | • | |
| 2.D.02 Use familiar language | | • | • | • | • | • | • | • | • |
| 2.D.03 Verbal and non-verbal communication | | • | • | • | • | • | • | • | • |
| 2.D.04 Develop vocabulary | | • | • | • | • | • | • | • | • |
| (There is no 2.D.05 in draft) | | | | | | | | | |
| 2.D.06 Solve problems | | • | • | • | • | • | | • | • |
| **2.E Early Literacy** | | | | | | | | | |
| 2.E.01 and 2.E.02Experience songs, rhymes, games, books | | | | | | | | | • |
| 2.E.03 Become familiar with print | | • | | | | | | | • |
| 2.E.04 Read or be read to | | | | | | • | | | |
| 2.E.05 Write or dictate | | | | | | | | | • |
| 2.E.07 Recognize and write letters | | | | | | | | | • |
| 2.E.08 Access books and writing materials | | | | | | | | | |
| 2.E.09 Read familiar words and sentences | | | | | | | | | • |
| 2.E.10 Identify phonemes | | | | | | | | | |
| 2.E.11 Write independently | | | | | | | | | |

| Observe | | | | | | Let's Make Something | | | | | | | | Let's Measure | | | |
| Clouds | Behaviour of Living Things | Biodiversity | Effects of Wind | Bird Watching | The Garden at Night | Using Plants as Art Tools | Falling Leaves and Bits of Bark | Preparing Lunch | Seed Design | Drawing Shadows | Making a Collage | Discovering Textures | Arranging Bouquets | Comparing Plants | Shapes | Nature's Geometry | How Many and How Big |
|---|---|---|---|---|---|---|---|---|---|---|---|---|---|---|---|---|---|
| • | • | • | • | • | • | • | • | • | • | • | • | • | • | • | • | • | • |
| • | • |   | • | • | • | • | • | • | • | • | • | • | • |   |   | • |   |
| • |   | • |   | • | • |   | • | • |   | • |   | • | • | • |   |   |   |
|   | • |   | • |   | • |   |   |   |   |   | • |   | • |   | • | • | • |
|   |   |   |   |   |   |   |   | • |   |   | • | • |   | • |   |   |   |
|   |   |   |   |   |   |   |   | • | • |   | • | • |   |   |   | • |   |
|   | • |   | • |   |   |   |   | • | • |   | • | • |   |   | • | • | • |
| • |   |   |   |   |   |   |   |   |   |   |   | • | • |   |   |   |   |
| • | • | • | • |   | • |   | • | • | • | • | • | • | • | • | • | • | • |
|   |   | • |   |   |   | • | • | • | • | • | • | • | • |   |   |   |   |
|   |   | • |   |   |   | • | • |   |   | • | • | • |   |   |   |   | • |
|   | • |   | • |   |   |   | • |   |   | • | • | • |   | • | • | • | • |
| • | • | • |   | • |   | • | • | • | • | • |   | • |   | • | • | • | • |
| • | • | • | • | • | • | • | • | • | • | • | • | • | • | • | • | • | • |
| • | • | • | • | • | • | • | • | • | • | • | • | • | • | • | • | • | • |
| • | • | • | • | • | • | • | • | • | • | • | • | • | • | • | • | • | • |
| • | • | • | • |   | • | • | • | • | • |   | • |   | • | • | • | • | • |
|   |   |   |   |   |   |   |   |   |   |   |   |   |   |   |   |   |   |
|   |   |   |   |   |   |   |   |   |   |   |   |   |   |   |   |   |   |
| • |   | • |   |   |   |   |   | • | • |   |   |   |   | • |   |   |   |
|   |   |   |   |   |   |   |   |   |   |   |   | • |   |   |   |   |   |
|   |   | • |   |   |   | • | • | • | • |   |   |   |   | • | • |   |   |
|   |   | • |   |   |   |   |   | • | • |   |   |   |   | • |   |   |   |
|   |   |   |   |   |   |   |   |   |   |   |   |   |   |   |   |   |   |
| • |   | • |   |   |   |   |   | • | • |   |   |   |   | • |   |   |   |
|   |   |   | • |   |   |   |   |   |   |   |   |   |   |   |   |   |   |
|   |   |   |   |   |   |   |   |   |   |   |   |   |   |   | • | • | • |

| Things to do | Let's Make Music | | | | | Let's Make | | |
|---|---|---|---|---|---|---|---|---|
| | The Food Chain Song | Nature's Band | Musical Gourds | Listening in the Garden | Songs of Nature | The Leaf Fairy | Playing House and Playing Store | Hollyhock Dolls |
| **Children have opportunities to** | | | | | | | | |
| **2.B Social-Emotional Development** | • | • | • | • | • | • | • | • |
| 1. Relate to others | • | • | • | • | | • | • | • |
| 2. Express Feelings | | • | • | • | • | | | • |
| 3. Learn Skills | | | | | • | | • | |
| 4. Develop confidence | • | • | • | | • | | • | • |
| 5. Enter social groups | • | • | • | | • | | • | |
| 6. Copperate | • | • | • | | • | | | • |
| 7. Develop Empathy | | | | | | | • | |
| **2.C Physical Development** | | | | | | | | |
| 1. move freely | | • | • | | • | | • | |
| 2. use fingers and hands | | | • | | | • | • | • |
| 3. develop fine motor | | • | • | | | • | • | |
| 4. Have large motor experiences | | • | • | • | • | | | • |
| **2.D Language Development** | | | | | | | | |
| 2.D.01 Align with learning environment | • | • | | • | • | • | • | |
| 2.D.02 Use familiar language | • | • | • | • | • | • | • | |
| 2.D.03 Verbal and non-verbal communication | • | • | • | | • | | • | • |
| 2.D.04 Develop vocabulary | • | • | • | • | • | • | • | • |
| (There is no 2.D.05 in draft) | | | | | | | | |
| 2.D.06 Solve problems | | • | | • | • | | • | |
| **2.E Early Literacy** | | | | | | | | |
| 2.E.01 and 2.E.02 Experience songs, rhymes, games, books | • | • | • | • | • | • | | • |
| 2.E.03 Become familiar with print | | | • | • | | | | |
| 2.E.04 Read or be read to | | | • | | | | | |
| 2.E.05 Write or dictate | • | • | • | • | • | | | |
| 2.E.07 Recognize and write letters | | | • | • | | | | |
| 2.E.08 Access books and writing materials | | | | | | | | |
| 2.E.09 Read familiar words and sentences | | | • | • | | | | |
| 2.E.10 Identify phonemes | • | | | | • | | | |
| 2.E.11 Write independently | | | | | • | • | | |

| | Believe | | | Let's Play a Game | | | | | Let's Enjoy Winter | | | | | |
| --- | --- | --- | --- | --- | --- | --- | --- | --- | --- | --- | --- | --- | --- | --- |
| | Leaf Money | Imitating Animals | Moving with the Wind | Finger Play | Pretending to be a Plant or Animal | Playing with Dandelions | Playing with Shadows | Enjoying Garden Poetry | Playing in the Snow | Gathering Food in the Winter | Tracks in the Snow | Watching Winter Birds | Looking Closely at Ice and Snow | Trees and Twigs |
| | • | • | • | • | • | • | • | • | • | • | • | • | • | • |
| | • | • | • | | • | • | | • | • | • | • | • | • | • |
| | | • | | • | | | • | | • | • | | • | • | • |
| | | | • | | • | | | | • | | | | | |
| | • | • | • | | • | • | • | | • | • | • | | | |
| | | • | • | • | • | • | • | • | • | • | | | | |
| | | | | | • | | | • | • | • | | | | |
| | | | | | • | | | | | | | • | • | • |
| | | • | • | | | • | • | | • | • | • | • | • | • |
| | • | | • | | | • | | | | | | | | • |
| | • | | • | | | | | | | | | | | |
| | | • | • | • | | | • | | • | • | • | | | |
| | • | • | • | • | • | • | • | • | | | | | | |
| | • | • | • | • | • | • | • | • | • | • | | | | |
| | • | • | | • | • | • | • | • | • | | | • | • | • |
| | • | • | • | • | • | • | • | • | • | • | • | • | • | • |
| | • | • | | | • | • | • | • | • | • | • | • | • | • |
| | • | | • | • | • | • | • | • | • | | • | | | |
| | | • | • | • | | | | | | | | | | |
| | | | | | | | | | • | | | | | |
| | | | | | | | | | | | | | | |
| | | | | | | • | | | | | | | | |
| | | | | • | | | | • | | | | | | |
| | | | | | | • | | | | | | | | |

| Appendix D.2.a<br><br>NAEYC Criteria for Mathematics.<br>Children are provided opportunities to: / Things to do | Let's Explore | | | | | Let's | | |
|---|---|---|---|---|---|---|---|---|
| | Home of Animals | Pond Life | Insects Flying on Gossamer | Spider Webs | Will It Rain Soon? | The Garden Air | Interesting Little Stones | Playing with Dirt |
| 2.F Use language, gestures, and materials to convey mathematical concepts such as more and less and big and small. | • | • | • | • | • | • | • | • |
| See and touch different shapes, sizes, colors, and patterns | • | • | • | • | • | | • | • |
| Read books that include counting and shapes | | • | | | | | | |
| 2.F.02 Build understanding of numbers, number names, and their relationship to object quantities and to symbols. | | • | | • | • | | • | • |
| 2.F.03 Categorize by one or two attributes such as shape, size and color | • | • | • | | • | | | • |
| 2.F.04 Integrate mathematical terms into everyday conversation | • | • | • | • | • | • | • | • |
| 2.F.05 Understand the concepts of measurement by using standard and non-standard units of measurement | | | | | | | • | • |
| 2.F.06 Understand basic concepts of geometry by, for example, naming and recognizing two and three-dimensional shapes and recognizing how figures are composed of different shapes. | • | • | | • | • | | • | • |
| 2.F.07 Build an understanding of time in the context of their lives, schedules and routines | | | | | • | | • | |
| 2.F.08 Recognize and name repeating patterns | | | • | • | | • | | |
| 2.F.09 Use standard and non-standard units of measurement and assign numerical values to measurements | | | | | • | • | • | |
| 2.F.10 Create, represent , discuss and extend repeating and growing patterns | | | | • | | | | |
| 2.F.11 Use written mathematical representations in everyday experiences | • | | | | | | • | |
| 2.F.12 Use numerical symbols and to explore operations on quantities, such as adding, taking away, and dividing into equal and unequal subsets | | • | | • | • | | • | • |
| 2.F.13 Use conventional tools such as a calendar and a clock for understanding time. | | • | | | • | | | |

| | Observe | | | | | | Let's Make Something | | | | | | | | Let's Measure | | | |
|---|---|---|---|---|---|---|---|---|---|---|---|---|---|---|---|---|---|---|
| | Clouds | Behaviour of Living Things | Biodiversity | Effects of Wind | Bird Watching | The Garden at Night | Using Plants as Art Tools | Falling Leaves and Bits of Bark | Preparing Lunch | Seed Design | Drawing Shadows | Making a Collage | Discovering Textures | Arranging Bouquets | Comparing Plants | Shapes | Nature's Geometry | How Many and How Big |
| | • | | • | • | • | • | • | • | • | • | • | • | • | | • | • | • | • |
| | • | • | • | • | • | • | • | • | • | • | • | • | • | • | • | • | • | • |
| | | | • | • | | | • | • | • | | | | • | | | | | |
| | | | • | | • | | • | • | • | • | • | • | • | | | | • | • |
| | • | • | • | | • | | • | • | • | • | • | • | • | • | | • | • | • |
| | | | • | | • | • | • | • | • | • | • | • | | | • | • | • | • |
| | | | | | • | | • | • | • | • | • | | • | | • | • | | • |
| | | | • | | • | | • | • | • | • | • | • | • | • | | • | • | • |
| | | | | | | | | | | | | | | | | | | |
| | | • | | | • | | • | | | | | | | | • | | • | |
| | | | • | • | • | • | • | • | • | • | • | | | | • | | | • |
| | | | • | | • | | • | | | • | | | | | | | | |
| | | | • | | • | | | | • | | • | | | | | | | |
| | | | | | | | | | | | | | | | | | | |
| | | | | | | | | | | | | | | | | | | • |

| Things to do | Let's Make Music | | | | | Let's Make | | |
|---|---|---|---|---|---|---|---|---|
| Appendix D.2.b<br><br>NAEYC Criteria for Mathematics.<br>Children are provided opportunities to: | The Food Chain Song | Nature's Band | Musical Gourds | Listening in the Garden | Songs of Nature | The Leaf Fairy | Playing House and Playing Store | Hollyhock Dolls |
| 2.F Use language, gestures, and materials to convey mathematical concepts such as more and less and big and small. | • | • | • | • | • | • | • | • |
| See and touch different shapes, sizes, colors, and patterns | | • | • | • | • | • | • | • |
| Read books that include counting and shapes | | | • | | | | | |
| 2.F.02 Build understanding of numbers, number names, and their relationship to object quantities and to symbols. | | • | • | | | | | |
| 2.F.03 Categorize by one or two attributes such as shape, size and color | • | • | • | | | • | • | • |
| 2.F.04 Integrate mathematical terms into everyday conversation | | | • | | • | • | • | • |
| 2.F.05 Understand the concepts of measurement by using standard and non-standard units of measurement | | | • | | | • | | |
| 2.F.06 Understand basic concepts of geometry by, for example, naming and recognizing two and three-dimensional shapes and recognizing how figures are composed of different shapes. | | • | | | | | • | |
| 2.F.07 Build an understanding of time in the context of their lives, schedules and routines | | | | | | | | |
| 2.F.08 Recognize and name repeating patterns | | • | • | | • | | | |
| 2.F.09 Use standard and non-standard units of measurement and assign numerical values to measurements | | | | • | • | • | | |
| 2.F.10 Create, represent , discuss and extend repeating and growing patterns | | | | | • | | | • |
| 2.F.11 Use written mathematical representations in everyday experiences | | | | | | | | |
| 2.F.12 Use numerical symbols and to explore operations on quantities, such as adding, taking away, and dividing into equal and unequal subsets | | | • | | | | | |
| 2.F.13 Use conventional tools such as a calendar and a clock for understanding time. | | | • | | | | | |

| | Believe | | | Let's Play a Game | | | | | Let's Enjoy Winter | | | | | |
|---|---|---|---|---|---|---|---|---|---|---|---|---|---|---|
| | Leaf Money | Imitating Animals | Moving with the Wind | Finger Play | Pretending to be a Plant or Animal | Playing with Dandelions | Playing with Shadows | Enjoying Garden Poetry | Playing in the Snow | Gathering Food in the Winter | Tracks in the Snow | Watching Winter Birds | Looking Closely at Ice and Snow | Trees and Twigs |
| | • | • | • | • | | • | • | | • | • | • | • | • | • |
| | • | • | • | • | • | • | • | | • | • | • | • | • | • |
| | | • | • | | | | | | | | | | | |
| | | | | • | | • | | | • | • | | • | • | • |
| | • | • | • | • | • | • | | | • | • | • | • | • | • |
| | | | | • | | | • | | • | • | | • | • | • |
| | | | | | • | | • | | | | | • | • | • |
| | • | • | | | | | | | | | • | | • | • |
| | | | | | | | | | | | | | | |
| | | | | | | | | • | | | • | | | • |
| | | | | | | | | | | | | • | | • |
| | | | | | | | | • | | | | | • | |
| | | | | | | | | | | | | | | |
| | | | | | | | | | | | | | | |
| | | | | | | | • | | • | | | | | |

163

| Appendix D.3.a<br><br>NAEYC Criteria for Science | **Things to do** | Let's Explore | | | | Let's | | | |
|---|---|---|---|---|---|---|---|---|---|
| | | Home of Animals | Pond Life | Insects Flying on Gossamer | Spider Webs | Will It Rain Soon? | The Garden Air | Interesting Little Stones | Playing with Dirt |
| 2.G.01 Use their senses to learn about objects in the environment, discover that they can make things happen and solve simple problems | | • | • | • | • | • | • | • | • |
| 2.G.02 Learn key content and principles of science such as<br>*the difference between living and nonliving things (e.g. plants versus rocks) and life cycles of various organisms (e.g., plants, butterflies, humans) | | • | • | • | • | | | | |
| * earth and sky (e.g., season; weather; geological features; light and shadow; sun, moon and stars). | | | | | | • | | | • |
| * structure and property of matter (e.g., characteristics that include concepts such as hard and soft, floating and sinking) and behavior of materials (e.g., transformation of liquids and solids by dissolving or melting). | | • | • | • | | • | • | • | • |
| 2.G.03 Use of the five sense to observe, explore and experiment with scientific phenomena | | • | • | • | • | • | • | • | • |
| 2.G.04 Use simple tools to observe objects and scientific phenomena | | • | • | | • | • | | • | • |
| 2.G.05 Collect data and to represent and document their findings (e.g., through drawing or graphing). | | • | • | • | • | • | | • | • |
| 2.G.06 Think, question, and reason about observed and inferred phenomena. | | • | • | • | • | • | • | • | • |
| 2.G.07 Discuss scientific concepts in everyday conversation. | | • | • | • | • | • | • | • | • |
| 2.G.08 Learn and use scientific terminology and vocabulary associated with the content areas. | | • | | • | • | • | • | • | • |

| Observe | | | | | | Let's Make Something | | | | | | | | Let's Measure | | | |
| --- | --- | --- | --- | --- | --- | --- | --- | --- | --- | --- | --- | --- | --- | --- | --- | --- | --- |
| Clouds | Behaviour of Living Things | Biodiversity | Effects of Wind | Bird Watching | The Garden at Night | Using Plants as Art Tools | Falling Leaves and Bits of Bark | Preparing Lunch | Seed Design | Drawing Shadows | Making a Collage | Discovering Textures | Arranging Bouquets | Comparing Plants | Shapes | Nature's Geometry | How Many and How Big |
| • | • | • | • | • | • | • | • | • | • | • | • | • | • | • | • | • | • |
|  | • | • | • | • | • |  |  | • | • | • |  | • | • | • | • | • | • |
|  |  |  | • | • | • |  |  |  |  | • |  |  |  |  |  |  | • |
| • |  | • |  |  |  | • | • | • | • |  |  | • | • | • | • | • | • |
|  |  | • | • |  | • | • | • | • | • | • |  | • | • | • | • |  | • |
| • |  |  | • | • |  | • | • | • |  |  | • | • | • |  | • |  | • |
|  | • | • |  | • |  | • | • | • | • | • | • | • |  | • | • | • | • |
| • | • | • | • | • | • | • | • | • | • | • | • | • | • | • | • | • | • |
| • | • | • | • | • |  | • | • | • | • | • | • | • | • | • | • | • | • |
|  | • | • | • | • | • | • |  | • | • |  | • | • | • | • | • | • | • |

| Appendix D.3.b<br><br>NAEYC Criteria for Science | Things to do | Let's Make Music | | | | | Let's Make | | |
|---|---|---|---|---|---|---|---|---|---|
| | | The Food Chain Song | Nature's Band | Musical Gourds | Listening in the Garden | Songs of Nature | The Leaf Fairy | Playing House and Playing Store | Hollyhock Dolls |
| 2.G.01 Use their senses to learn about objects in the environment, discover that they can make things happen and solve simple problems | | | • | • | • | • | • | • | • |
| 2.G.02 Learn key content and principles of science such as<br>*the difference between living and nonliving things (e.g. plants versus rocks) and life cycles of various organisms (e.g., plants, butterflies, humans) | | • | • | • | • | • | | | • |
| * earth and sky (e.g., season; weather; geological features; light and shadow; sun, moon and stars). | | • | | | | | | • | |
| * structure and property of matter (e.g., characteristics that include concepts such as hard and soft, floating and sinking) and behavior of materials (e.g., transformation of liquids and solids by dissolving or melting). | | | • | | • | • | | • | |
| 2.G.03 Use of the five sense to observe, explore and experiment with scientific phenomena | | | • | • | | | | | |
| 2.G.04 Use simple tools to observe objects and scientific phenomena | | | • | | | • | • | | |
| 2.G.05 Collect data and to represent and document their findings (e.g., through drawing or graphing). | | • | • | • | • | • | • | | • |
| 2.G.06 Think, question, and reason about observed and inferred phenomena. | | | • | • | • | • | | | |
| 2.G.07 Discuss scientific concepts in everyday conversation. | | • | • | • | • | | | | |
| 2.G.08 Learn and use scientific terminology and vocabulary associated with the content areas. | | • | • | • | • | • | | | • |

| | Believe | | | Let's Play a Game | | | | | Let's Enjoy Winter | | | | | |
|---|---|---|---|---|---|---|---|---|---|---|---|---|---|---|
| | Leaf Money | Imitating Animals | Moving with the Wind | Finger Play | Pretending to be a Plant or Animal | Playing with Dandelions | Playing with Shadows | Enjoying Garden Poetry | Playing in the Snow | Gathering Food in the Winter | Tracks in the Snow | Watching Winter Birds | Looking Closely at Ice and Snow | Trees and Twigs |
| | • | • | • | • | • | • | • | • | • | • | • | • | • | • |
| | | • | | | | • | | | • | | | • | | • |
| | | | | | | | • | | • | • | • | • | • | • |
| | | | • | | | | | | • | • | | | • | |
| | | | | | | | • | | • | • | | • | | |
| | | | | | | | • | | • | • | | | • | |
| | • | | • | | • | | • | • | | | • | • | • | • |
| | | • | • | • | | • | • | | | • | • | • | • | • |
| | | • | | | • | • | • | | • | • | • | • | • | • |
| | • | | • | | | • | • | | • | • | | • | • | • |

| Things to do | Let's Explore | | | | | Let's | |
| --- | --- | --- | --- | --- | --- | --- | --- |
| **Appendix D.4.a**<br><br>NAEYC Curriculum Criteria for The Arts, Health and Safety, Social Studies | Home of Animals | Pond Life | Insects Flying on Gossamer | Spider Webs | Will It Rain Soon? | The Garden Air | Interesting Little Stones |
| **2.J. Creative Expression and the Arts, Children are provided opportunities for:** | | | | | | | |
| 2.J.0 Art, music, drama, and dance that reflect cultural diversity | | | | | | | |
| 2.J.04 Learn new concepts and vocabulary related to art, music, drama, and dance. | | • | • | | • | | |
| 2.J.05 Cutting, gluing, and caring for tools. | | | | | • | | |
| 2.J.06 Music, drama, dance, and two- and three-dimensional art | • | • | • | • | • | | • |
| 2.J.07 Respond to the art of other children and adults. | • | • | • | • | • | | |
| **2.K Health and Safety** | | | | | | | |
| 2.K.01 Good health practices | | | • | | • | • | |
| 2.K.02 Nutrition, sources of food and recognizing, preparing, eating, and valuing healthy foods. | | | | | | | |
| 2.K.03 and 2.K.04 Safety rules and procedures. | • | • | • | • | | | |
| **2.L Cognitive Development: Social Studies** | | | | | | | |
| 2.L.01 Positive identity and an emerging sense of self and others. | | | | | • | | |
| 2.L.02 Feels accepted and gains a sense of belonging in community. | | | | | | • | |
| 2.L.03 Diversity in non-stereotypical ways. | • | • | • | | | | |
| 2.L.04 Social roles in the family and workplace through play. | | | | | | | |
| 2.L.05 T P K Community in which they live | | | | | | • | |
| 2.L.06 Fairness, friendship, responsibility, authority, and differences. | | | • | • | | | |
| 2.L.07 Geography | | | | | | | |
| 2.L.08 and 2.L.09 Care for the environment. | • | • | • | • | | • | |
| 2.L.10 Economic concepts | | | | | | | |
| 2.L.11 Hometown, state, the United States and their country of origin | | | | | | • | |

| Observe | | | | | | | Let's Make Something | | | | | | | | Let's Measure | | | |
|---|---|---|---|---|---|---|---|---|---|---|---|---|---|---|---|---|---|---|
| Playing with Dirt | Clouds | Behaviour of Living Things | Biodiversity | Effects of Wind | Bird Watching | The Garden at Night | Using Plants as Art Tools | Falling Leaves and Bits of Bark | Preparing Lunch | Seed Design | Drawing Shadows | Making a Collage | Discovering Textures | Arranging Bouquets | Comparing Plants | Shapes | Nature's Geometry | How Many and How Big |
|  |  |  |  |  |  |  |  |  |  |  |  |  |  |  |  |  |  |  |
|  |  |  |  | ● |  |  | ● | ● |  |  |  |  |  |  |  |  |  |  |
|  |  | ● | ● |  |  |  |  |  |  |  | ● |  | ● |  |  | ● | ● | ● |
|  |  | ● |  |  |  |  | ● |  |  | ● |  | ● | ● |  |  |  |  |  |
|  |  | ● | ● | ● | ● |  | ● | ● |  |  | ● | ● |  | ● | ● | ● | ● | ● |
|  |  | ● |  |  |  |  | ● | ● |  |  | ● | ● | ● | ● |  |  | ● |  |
|  |  |  |  | ● | ● | ● |  |  | ● |  |  |  |  |  |  |  |  |  |
| ● |  |  |  |  |  |  |  |  |  |  |  | ● | ● |  |  |  |  |  |
|  |  |  |  |  |  |  | ● | ● | ● |  |  |  | ● |  |  |  |  |  |
|  |  |  |  |  |  |  |  |  |  |  |  |  |  |  |  |  |  |  |
| ● |  |  |  |  |  |  |  | ● | ● |  |  | ● | ● | ● |  |  |  |  |
| ● |  |  |  | ● |  | ● |  |  | ● |  |  | ● | ● |  | ● |  | ● |  |
|  |  | ● | ● | ● | ● |  |  |  | ● | ● |  |  |  |  |  |  |  |  |
|  |  | ● |  |  | ● | ● |  |  | ● | ● | ● | ● |  |  |  |  |  |  |
|  |  |  |  |  |  | ● |  |  | ● |  | ● |  |  | ● |  |  |  |  |
|  |  |  |  |  | ● |  | ● | ● | ● | ● |  | ● |  | ● |  |  |  |  |
|  |  | ● |  | ● |  |  |  |  |  |  | ● | ● |  |  |  |  |  |  |
|  |  | ● | ● |  | ● |  | ● | ● |  |  |  |  | ● |  | ● |  |  |  |
|  |  |  |  |  |  |  |  |  |  |  |  |  |  |  |  |  |  |  |
|  |  |  |  |  |  |  | ● | ● |  |  |  |  |  |  |  |  |  |  |

| Things to do | Let's Make Music | | | | | Let's Make | | |
|---|---|---|---|---|---|---|---|---|
| **Appendix D.4.b**<br><br>NAEYC Curriculum Criteria for The Arts, Health and Safety, Social Studies | The Food Chain Song | Nature's Band | Musical Gourds | Listening in the Garden | Songs of Nature | The Leaf Fairy | Playing House and Playing Store | Hollyhock Dolls |
| **2.J. Creative Expression and the Arts, Children are provided opportunities for:** | | | | | | | | |
| 2.J.0 Art, music, drama, and dance that reflect cultural diversity | • | • | • | | • | • | • | • |
| 2.J.04 Learn new concepts and vocabulary related to art, music, drama, and dance. | • | • | • | | | • | | • |
| 2.J.05 Cutting, gluing, and caring for tools. | | | • | | | | | |
| 2.J.06 Music, drama, dance, and two- and three-dimensional art | • | • | • | • | | • | | • |
| 2.J.07 Respond to the art of other children and adults. | | | • | • | | • | | • |
| **2.K Health and Safety** | | | | | | | | |
| 2.K.01 Good health practices | • | | • | | | • | | |
| 2.K.02 Nutrition, sources of food and recognizing, preparing, eating, and valuing healthy foods. | | | • | | | | | |
| 2.K.03 and 2.K.04 Safety rules and procedures. | | | | | | • | | • |
| **2.L Cognitive Development: Social Studies** | | | | | | | | |
| 2.L.01 Positive identity and an emerging sense of self and others. | | • | • | • | • | | | • |
| 2.L.02 Feels accepted and gains a sense of belonging in community. | | • | • | | • | • | • | |
| 2.L.03 Diversity in non-stereotypical ways. | | • | | | | | • | • |
| 2.L.04 Social roles in the family and workplace through play. | | | | | | | | |
| 2.L.05 T P K Community in which they live | • | | | • | • | • | • | |
| 2.L.06 Fairness, friendship, responsibility, authority, and differences. | • | • | • | | | • | • | |
| 2.L.07 Geography | | | | | | | | |
| 2.L.08 and 2.L.09 Care for the environment. | • | | | | • | • | | |
| 2.L.10 Economic concepts | | | | | | | • | |
| 2.L.11 Hometown, state, the United States and their country of origin | | • | | | | | | |

| Believe | | | Let's Play a Game | | | | | Let's Enjoy Winter | | | | | |
|---|---|---|---|---|---|---|---|---|---|---|---|---|---|
| Leaf Money | Imitating Animals | Moving with the Wind | Finger Play | Pretending to Be a Plant or Animal | Playing with Dandelions | Playing with Shadows | Enjoying Garden Poetry | Playing in the Snow | Gathering Food in the Winter | Tracks in the Snow | Watching Winter Birds | Looking Closely at Ice and Snow | Trees and Twigs |
| • | • | • |  | • |  |  | • | • | • |  |  |  |  |
|  | • | • | • | • |  |  | • |  |  |  |  | • |  |
| • | • | • | • | • |  |  |  | • |  |  |  | • |  |
| • | • |  |  | • |  |  |  |  |  |  |  | • |  |
|  | • | • | • |  |  |  |  | • | • | • |  | • |  |
|  |  |  |  |  | • |  |  |  | • |  |  |  |  |
| • |  |  |  | • |  |  |  | • | • | • |  |  | • |
| • | • | • |  |  | • |  | • | • |  | • |  |  |  |
|  | • | • | • |  |  |  |  | • | • | • |  |  |  |
| • |  | • |  | • |  |  | • | • |  |  |  |  |  |
|  |  |  |  |  | • |  |  | • | • | • | • |  |  |
|  |  |  |  |  |  |  |  |  |  | • |  |  |  |
|  |  |  |  |  | • |  |  | • |  | • |  |  | • |
|  |  |  |  | • |  |  |  |  | • |  |  |  |  |
| • |  |  |  | • |  |  | • | • | • | • | • | • | • |

# Index

# V

# W

CPSIA information can be obtained at www.ICGtesting.com
Printed in the USA
LVOW12s1209120214

373383LV00002B/696/P